MEASURING TOOLS

Edited by
MD. ANAMUL HASAN
B. Sc in Mechanical Engineering, KUET
CAD Engineer, BJIT Ltd
Former Design Engineer, Plastic Product Design,
Pran RFL Group

Pink
Dots

PINK . DOTS
2020

MEASURING TOOLS
MD. ANAMUL HASAN

Categorie(s): Machinery's Reference, Engineering, Mechanical

For Any Question & Customer Service:

Email us at: pinkdotsbd@gmail.com

Title the email "PINK . DOTS - Book Name" and let us get your feedback.

Copyright © PINK . DOTS

All rights reserved. No part of this publication may be reproduced, distributed, or transmitted in any form or by any means, including photocopying, recording, or other electronic or mechanical methods, without the prior written permission.

ISBN-13: 979-8632295550

MEASURING TOOLS

CONTENTS

	Title	Page No
CHAPTER I	HISTORY AND DEVELOPMENT OF STANDARD MEASUREMENTS	5 - 15
CHAPTER II	CALIPERS, DIVIDERS, AND SURFACE GAGES	16 - 31
CHAPTER III	MICROMETER MEASURING INSTRUMENTS	32 – 58
CHAPTER IV	MISCELLANEOUS MEASURING TOOLS AND GAGES	59 – 70
	NOTES	71 - 72

CHAPTER I
HISTORY AND DEVELOPMENT OF STANDARD MEASUREMENTS [1]

While every mechanic makes use of the standards of length every day, and uses tools graduated according to accepted standards when performing even the smallest operation in the shop, there are comparatively few who know the history of the development of the standard measurements of length, or are familiar with the methods employed in transferring the measurements from the reference standard to the working standards. We shall therefore here give a short review of the history and development of standard measurements of length, as abstracted from a paper read by Mr. W. A. Viall before the Providence Association of Mechanical Engineers.

Origin of Standard Measurements

By examining the ruins of the ancients, it has been found that they had standard measurements, not in the sense in which we are now to consider them, but the ruins show that the buildings were constructed according to some regular unit. In many, if not all cases, the unit seems to be some part of the human body. The "foot," it is thought, first appeared in Greece, and the standard was traditionally said to have been received from the foot of Hercules, and a later tradition has it that Charlemagne established the measurement of his own foot as the standard for his country.

Standards Previous to 1800

In England, prior to the conquest, the yard measured, according to later investigations, 39.6 inches, but it was reduced by Henry I in 1101, to compare with the measurement of his own arm. In 1324, under Edward II, it was enacted that "the inch shall have length of three barley corns, round and dry, laid end to end; twelve inches shall make one foot, and three feet one yard." While this standard for measurement was the accepted one, scientists were at work on a plan to establish a standard for length that could be recovered if lost, and Huygens, a noted philosopher and scientist of his day, suggested that the pendulum, which beats according to its length, should be used to establish the units of measurement. In 1758 Parliament appointed a commission to investigate and compare the various standards with that furnished by the Royal Society. The commission caused a copy of this standard to be made, marked it "Standard Yard, 1758," and laid it before the House of Commons. In 1742, members of the Royal Society of England and the Royal Academy of Science of Paris agreed to exchange standards, and two bars 42 inches long, with three feet marked off upon them, were sent to Paris, and one of these was returned later with "Toise" marked upon it. In 1760 a yard bar was prepared by Mr. Bird, which was afterwards adopted as a standard, as we shall see later.

In 1774 the Royal Society offered a reward of a hundred guineas for a method that would obtain an invariable standard, and Halton proposed a pendulum with a moving weight upon it, so that by counting the beats when the weight was in one position and again when in another, and then measuring the distance between the two positions, a distance could be defined that could at any time be duplicated. The Society paid 30 guineas for the suggestion, and later the work was taken up by J. Whitehurst with the result that the distance between the positions of the weight when vibrating 42 and 84 times a minute was 59.89358 inches. The method was not further developed.

How the Length of the Meter was Established

In 1790, Talleyrand, then Bishop of Autun, suggested to the Constituent Assembly that the king should endeavor to have the king of England request his parliament to appoint a commission to work in unison with one to be appointed in France, the same to be composed of members of the Royal Society and Royal Academy of Science, respectively, to determine the length of a pendulum beating seconds of time. England did not respond to the invitation, and the French commission appointed considered first of all whether the pendulum beating seconds of time, the quadrant of the meridian, or the quadrant of the equator should be determined as a source of the standard. It was decided that the quadrant of the meridian should be adopted and that 0.0000001 of it should be the standard.

The arc of about nine and one-half degrees, extending from Dunkirk on the English Channel to Barcelona on the Mediterranean and passing through Paris, should be the one to be measured. The actual work of measuring was done by Mechain and Delambre according to the plans laid down by the commission. Mechain was to measure about 25 per cent of the arc, the southern portion of it, and Delambre the remainder; the reason for this unequal division was that the northern division had been surveyed previously, and the territory was well-known, whereas the southern part was an unknown country, as far as the measurement of it went, and it was expected that many severe difficulties would have to be surmounted. The Revolution was in progress, and it was soon found that the perils attending the measurement of the northern part were greater than those attending the southern part of the territory. The people looked askance at all things that they did not understand, and Delambre with his instruments was looked upon as one sent to further enthrall them. He was set upon by the people at various times and although the authorities endeavored to protect him, it was only by his own bravery and tact that he was able to do his work and save his life. The Committee of Safety ordered that Mechain and Delambre close their work in 1795, and it was some time afterward before it was resumed.

Having completed the field work, the results of their labors were laid before a commission composed of members of the National Institute and learned men from other nations, who had accepted the invitation that had been extended to them, and after carefully reviewing and calculating the work, the length of the meridian was determined, and from it was established the meter as we now have it. A platinum bar was made according to the figures given, and this furnishes the prototype of the meter of the present time. Notwithstanding all of the care taken in establishing the meter, from work done by Gen. Schubert, of Russia, and Capt. Clarke, of England, it has been shown that it is not 0.0000001 of the quadrant passing through Paris, but of the one passing through New York.

The Standard Yard in England—Its Loss and Restoration

Whether incited by the work of the French or not, we do not know, but in the early part of this century the English began to do more work upon the establishment of a standard, and in 1816 a commission was appointed by the crown to examine and report upon the standard of length. Capt. Kater made a long series of careful observations determining the second pendulum to be 39.1386 inches when reduced to the level of the sea. This measurement was made on a scale made by Troughton—who, by the way, was the first to introduce the use of the microscope in making measurements—under the direction of and for Sir Geo. Schuckburgh. In 1822, having made three reports, after many tests, it was recommended that the standard prepared by Bird in 1760, marked "Standard Yard, 1760," be adopted as the standard for Great Britain.

The act of June, 1824, after declaring that this measure should be adopted as the standard, reads in Sec. III.: "And whereas it is expedient that the Standard Yard, if lost, destroyed, defaced or otherwise injured should be restored to the same length by reference to some invariable natural Standard; and whereas it has been ascertained by the Commissioners appointed by His Majesty to inquire into the Subjects of Weights and Measures, that the Yard, hereby declared to be the Imperial Standard Yard, when compared with a Pendulum vibrating Seconds of Mean Time in the latitude of London, in a Vacuum at the Level of the Sea, is in the proportion of Thirty-six Inches to Thirty-nine Inches and one thousand three hundred and ninety-three ten thousandth parts of an Inch; Be it enacted and declared, that if at any Time hereafter the said Imperial Standard Yard shall be lost, or shall be in any manner destroyed, defaced or otherwise injured, it shall and may be restored by making a new Standard Yard bearing the same proportion to such Pendulum, as aforesaid, as the said Imperial Standard Yard bears to such Pendulum."

It was not long after this act had been passed, if indeed not before, that it became known that the pendulum method was an incorrect one, as it was found that errors had occurred in reducing the length obtained to that at the sea level, and despite the great pains that had been taken, it is doubtful if the method was not faulty in some of its other details.

When the Houses of Parliament were burned in 1834, an opportunity was offered to try the method upon which so much time and care had been spent. A commission was appointed and to Sir Francis Baily was assigned the task of restoring the standard. He did not live to complete the task, dying in 1844. He succeeded in determining the composition of the metal that was best adapted to be used, which metal is now known as Baily's metal.

Rev. R. Sheepshanks constructed a working model as a standard and compared it with two Schuckburg's scales, the yard of the Royal Society, and two iron bars that had been used in the ordnance department. Having determined to his own satisfaction and that of his associates the value of the yard, he prepared the standard imperial yard, known as Bronze No. 1, a bronze bar $38 \times 1 \times 1$ inch, with two gold plugs dropped into holes so that the surface of the plugs passes through the center plane of the bar. Upon these plugs are three transverse lines and two longitudinal lines, the yard being the distance from the middle transverse line—the portion lying between the two longitudinal ones—of one plug, to the corresponding line on the other plug. Forty copies were made, but two of these being correct at 62 degrees Fahrenheit, and these two, together with the original and one other, are kept in England as the standards for reference. In 1855 the standard as made by Rev. Sheepshanks was legalized.

Attempts to Fix a Standard in the United States

The Constitution empowers Congress to fix the standards of weights and measures, but up to 1866 no legal standard length had been adopted. In his first message to Congress Washington said: "A uniformity in the weights and measures of the country is among the important objects submitted to you by the Constitution, and if it can be derived from a standard at once invariable and universal, it must be no less honorable to the public council than conducive to the public convenience."

In July, 1790, Thomas Jefferson, then Secretary of State, sent a report to Congress containing two plans, both based on the length of the pendulum, in this case the pendulum to be a plain bar, the one plan to use the system then existing, referring it to the pendulum as the basis, and the other to take the pendulum and subdivide it, one-third of the pendulum to be called a foot. The whole length was that of one beating seconds of time. He made a table to read as follows:

    10 Points make a Line.

    10 Lines make a Foot.

    10 Feet make a Decad.

    10 Decads make a Rood.

    10 Roods make a Furlong.

    10 Furlongs make a Mile.

Congress did not adopt his system, and as England was then working on the problem, it was decided to await the results of its labors. In 1816, Madison, in his inaugural address, brought the matter of standards to the attention of Congress, and a committee of the House made a report recommending the first plan of Jefferson, but the report was not acted upon. In 1821, J. Q. Adams, then Secretary of State, made a long and exhaustive report in which he favored the metric system, but still advised Congress to wait, and Congress—waited.

What the Standards are in the United States

The standard of length which had generally been accepted as the standard, was a brass scale 82 inches long, prepared by Troughton for the Coast Survey of the United States. The yard used was the 36 inches between the 27th and 63d inch of the scale. In 1856, however "Bronze No. 11" was presented to the United States by the British government. This is a duplicate of the No. 1 Bronze mentioned before, which is the legalized standard yard in England. It is standard length at 61.79 degrees F. and is the accepted standard in the United States. A bar of Low Moor iron, No. 57, was sent at the same time, and this is correct in length at 62.58 degrees F. The expansion of Bronze No. 11 is 0.000342 inch, and that of the iron bar is 0.000221 inch for each degree Fahrenheit. While the yard is the commonly accepted standard in this country, it is not the legal standard. In 1866 Congress passed a law making legal the meter, the first and only measure of length that has been legalized by our government. Copies of the meter and kilogram, taken from the original platinum bar at Paris, referred to before, were received in this country by the President and members of the Cabinet, on Jan. 2, 1890, and were deposited with the Coast Survey. By formal order of the Secretary of the Treasury, April 5, 1893, these were denominated the "Fundamental Standards."

The International Bureau of Weights and Measures

After the original meter was established, it was found that copies made by various countries differed to a greater or less extent from the original, and believing that a copy could be made from which other copies could be more readily made than from the end piece meter, and that better provision could be made for the preservation of the standard, France called a convention of representatives from various States using the system, to consider the matter. The United States representatives, or commissioners, were Messrs. Henry and Hildegard, who met with the general commission in 1870. The commissioners at once set at work to solve the problem presented to them, but the Franco-Prussian war put an end to their deliberations. The deliberations were resumed later, and May 20, 1875, representatives of the various countries signed a treaty providing for the establishment and maintenance, at the common expense of the contracting nations, of a "scientific and permanent international bureau of weights and measures, the location of which should be Paris, to be conducted by a general conference for weights and measures, to be composed of the delegates of all the contracting governments."

This bureau is empowered to construct and preserve the international standards, to distribute copies of the same to the several countries, and also to discuss and initiate measures necessary for the determination of the metric system. The commission adopted a form for the standard as shown in Fig. 1. The lines representing the length of the meter are drawn on the plane A, which is the neutral plane, and will not change in length should the bar deflect. The bar is made of 90 per cent platinum and 10 per cent iridium, about 250 kilograms having been melted when preparations were made for the first standard, so that all of the copies made from this cast represent the same coefficient of expansion and are subject to the same changes as the original. The French government presented to the bureau the pavilion Breteuil, opposite the Park of St. Cloud, which was accepted and put into order and is now the repository of the originals of the meter and the kilogram. The expense attending the first establishment of the bureau was about $10,000 to the United States, and since then its share of the annual expense has been about $900. The standards in the possession of the United States were received through the international bureau.

The Commercial Value of a Standard

Having at the disposal of the nation a standard of length, the question arises, "What can be made of it commercially, and how do we know when we have a copy of the standard?"

In 1893, the Brown & Sharpe Mfg. Co. decided to make a new standard to replace the one they had at that date. Mr. O. J. Beale was detailed to do this work. He prepared steel bars about 40 inches long by 1¼ inch square, and after planing them, they were allowed to rest for several months. At the ends of these bars he inserted two gold plugs, the centers of which were about 36 inches apart, and a little beyond these two others about one meter apart. A bar was placed in position upon a heavy bed.

MEASURING TOOLS

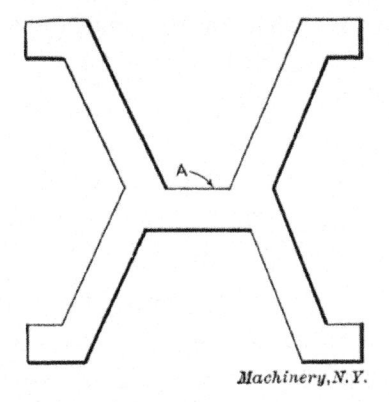

Fig. 1. Form of Bar Adopted for International Standards of Length

This was so arranged that a tool carrier could be passed over the bar. The tool carrier consisted of a light framework, holding the marking tool. One feature of the marking was that the point of the marking tool was curved and had an angle, so that if dropped it made an impression in the form of an ellipse. In graduations, ordinarily, the line, when highly magnified, is apt to present at its ends an impression less definite than in the center, by reason of the form of the objective. The line made with the tool mentioned is short, and that portion of the line is read which passes, apparently, through the straight line in the eyeglass of the microscope. In order to make these lines as definite as possible, the point was lapped to a bright surface. After being placed in position, the microscope, which could be placed on the front of the tool carrier, was set to compare with the graduation on the standard bar from which the new bar was to be prepared. After such a setting the readings were made by three persons, and by turning the lever the marking tool was dropped, making a very fine line, so fine indeed, that when the authorities in Washington began the examination of the bar later on they declared that no line had been made upon these studs.

After making the first line, the carriage was moved along to compare with the other line on the standard, and after the correction had been made by the use of the micrometer in the microscope, the marking tool was again dropped, giving the second line, which was intended to mark the limit of one yard over-all. The same operation was repeated in the marking of the meter. The whole of this work was done, of course, with the greatest care, and, while the theoretical portion of it appears very simple in detail, it required a great deal of time and patience before the last line had been made. The bar thus marked was taken to Washington, and in Mr. Beale's presence was compared by the attendants with Bronze No. 11 and later with Low Moor bar, No. 57.

In comparing this standard, a method was employed very similar to that used in marking it. The bar, properly supported, was placed upon a box that rested upon rolls, and on this same box was placed the government standard with which the Brown & Sharpe standard was to be compared. The standard was placed in position under the microscope, and after being properly set to the standard, the bar to be measured was placed under the microscope, and by the micrometer screw of the microscope the variation was measured. Three comparisons were made by each of the attendants on each end before determining the reading of the microscope, and after such comparisons and many repetitions of it, the value of the standard No. 2 was found to be 36.00061 inches for the yard, and 1.0000147 meter for the meter.

After this work had been done, Mr. Beale prepared a second standard which he called No. 3, and after examining, as shown above, the error was found to be 0.00002 inch for the yard, and 0.000005 meter for the meter. Observing these variations as compared with the standards originally made, we find they are very close, and it is doubtful if many repeated trials would furnish more accurate work, when we remember that out of forty original standards made, but two are correct at 62 degrees Fahrenheit.

After establishing a yard, the problem of obtaining an inch comes next, and this was made by subdividing the yard into two equal parts, these into three, and the three further subdivided into six parts. It should be particularly noted that no mention has been made of a standard inch, as there is none, the standard yard only existing, the subdivision of which falls upon those undertaking standard work. There is a remarkable agreement between at least three leading gage makers of this country and abroad, and each came to the result by its own method of subdividing the standard yard.

Kinds of Measurements and Measuring Tools

The measurements in the shop may, in general, be divided into measurements of length and measurements of angles. The length measurements in turn may be divided into line measurements and end measurements, the former being made by placing a rule or similar instrument against the object being measured, and comparing its length with the graduations on the measuring instruments; the latter are made by comparing the object being measured with the measuring instrument, by bringing the object measured into actual contact with the measuring surfaces of the instrument. Examples of line measurements are the ordinary measurements made with the machinist's rule, and examples of end measurement are those made by the micrometer, measuring machines, and snap gages. Angular measurements can also be divided into two classes; those measured directly by graduations on the instrument, and those measured by comparison with a given angle of the instrument.

Measuring instruments may also be divided into two classes, according to whether they actually are used for measuring, or whether they are principally used for comparing objects with one another. According to this classification all kinds of rules and protractors belong to the first class, whereas all gages belong to the second class. The ordinary instruments for length measurements, the regular machinists' rule, the caliper square, and the ordinary micrometer caliper, are too well known to require any additional explanation. The same is true of the regular bevel protractor for measuring angles. We shall therefore in the following chapters deal principally with special measuring tools, and with such methods in the use of tools which are likely to suggest improvements, or otherwise be valuable to the user and maker of measuring tools.

CHAPTER II
CALIPERS, DIVIDERS, AND SURFACE GAGES

In the present chapter we shall deal with the simpler forms of tools used for measuring, such as ordinary calipers, and their use; surface gages; special attachments for scales and squares, facilitating accurate measuring; and vernier and beam calipers. The descriptions of the tools and methods referred to have appeared in Machinery from time to time. The names of the persons who originally contributed these descriptions have been stated in notes at the foot of the pages, together with the month and year when their contribution appeared.

Setting Inside Calipers

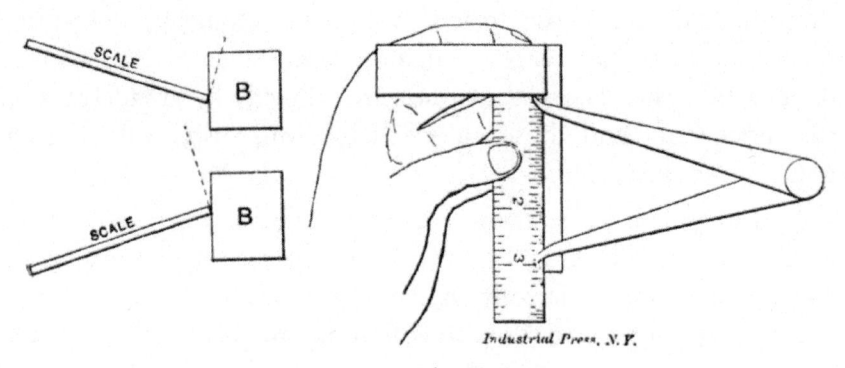

Figs. 2 and 3   Fig. 4
Setting Inside Calipers

It is customary with most machinists, when setting inside calipers to a scale, to place one end of the scale squarely against the face of some true surface, and then, placing one leg of the caliper against the same surface, to set the other leg to the required measurement on the scale. For this purpose, the faceplate of the lathe is frequently used on account of its being close at hand for the latheman. The sides of the jaws of a vise or almost anything located where the light is sufficient to read the markings on the scale are frequently used.

MEASURING TOOLS

The disadvantages of this method are, first, that a rough or untrue object is often chosen, particularly if it happens to be in a better light than a smooth and true one, and, second, that it is very hard to hold the scale squarely against an object. It is easy enough to hold it squarely crosswise, but it is not so easy a matter to keep it square edgewise. As can be readily seen, this makes quite a difference with the reading of the calipers, particularly if the scale is a thick one.

Figs. 2 and 3 show this effect exaggerated. B is the block against which the scale abuts. The dotted line indicates where the caliper leg should rest, but cannot do so, unless the scale is held perfectly square with the block. Fig. 4 shows a method of setting the calipers by using a small square to abut the scale and to afford a surface against which to place the leg of the caliper. The scale, lying flat on the blade of the square, is always sure to be square edgewise, and is easily held squarely against the stock of the square as shown. This method has also the advantage of being portable and can be taken to the window or to any place where the light is satisfactory. When using a long scale, the free end may be held against the body to assist in holding it in place.[2]

Shoulder Calipers

In Fig. 5 are shown a pair of calipers which are very handy in measuring work from shoulder to shoulder or from a shoulder to the end of the piece of work. For this purpose, they are much handier, and more accurate, than the ordinary "hermaphrodites." The legs are bent at AA so as to lie flat and thus bring the point of the long leg directly behind the short one which "nests" into it, as at B, so that the calipers may be used for short measurements as well as for long ones.

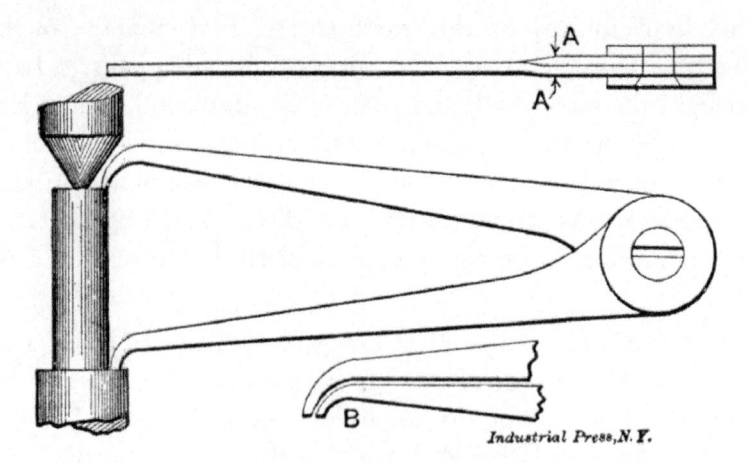

Fig. 5. Shoulder Calipers

Double-jointed Calipers to Fold in Toolbox

In Fig. 6 are illustrated a pair of large calipers that can be folded up and put in a machinist's ordinary size tool chest. The usual large caliper supplied by the average machine shop is so cumbersome and heavy that this one was designed to fill its place. It can be carried in the chest when the usual style of large caliper cannot. It is a very light and compact tool. It is a 26-inch caliper and will caliper up to 34 inches diameter. The top sections are made in four pieces, and the point ends fit between the top half like the blade of a knife, as shown in the engraving. Each side of the upper or top section is made of saw steel 1/16-inch-thick, and the lower part or point of steel ⅛ inch thick. The double section makes the tool very stiff and light.

The point section has a tongue A, extending between the double section, which is engaged by a sliding stud and thumb nut. The stud is a nice sliding fit in the slot, and the thumb nut clamps it firmly in place when in use. B, in the figure, shows the construction of the thumb nut. C is a sheet copper liner put between the washers at A. The dotted lines in the engraving show the points folded back to close up. The large joint washers are 1¾ inch diameter, and a ⅝-inch pin with a ⅜-inch hexagon head screw tightens it up. The forward joints are the same style, but smaller. The main joint has

MEASURING TOOLS

two 1¾-inch brass distance pieces or washers between the two main washers. The top section is 12½ inches between centers, and the point sections 15 inches from center to point. Closed up, the calipers measure 16 inches over-all.

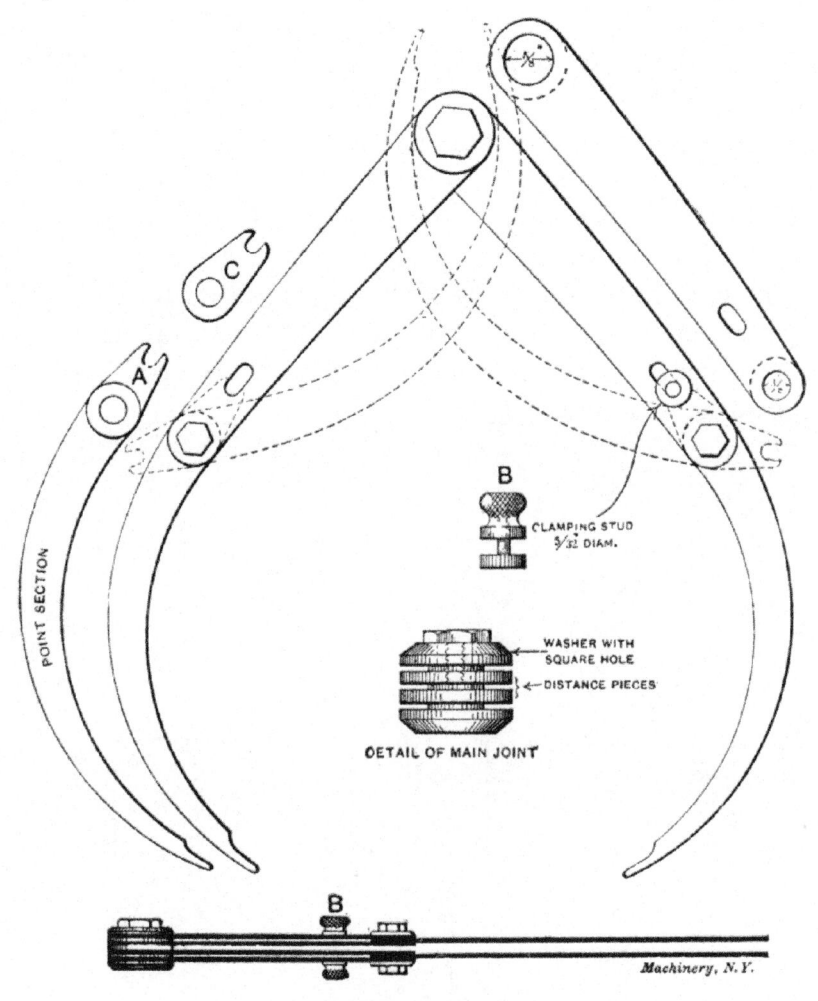

Fig. 6. Large Double-jointed Calipers

Kinks in Inside Calipering

Close measurements may be made by filing two notches in each leg of an inside caliper so as to leave a rounded projection between, as shown at E, Fig. 7. Then, with an outside caliper, D, the setting of the inside caliper, B, is taken from the rounded points. The inside caliper can be reset very accurately after removal by this method. A still better way is to have two short pins, CC' set in the sides of the inside caliper legs, but this is not readily done as a makeshift. To measure the inside diameter of a bore having a shoulder like the piece H, the inside caliper F may also be set as usual and then a line marked with a sharp scriber on one leg, by drawing it along the side G. Then the legs are closed to remove the caliper and are reset to the scribed line. Of course, this method is not as accurate as the previous one and can be used only for approximate measurements.

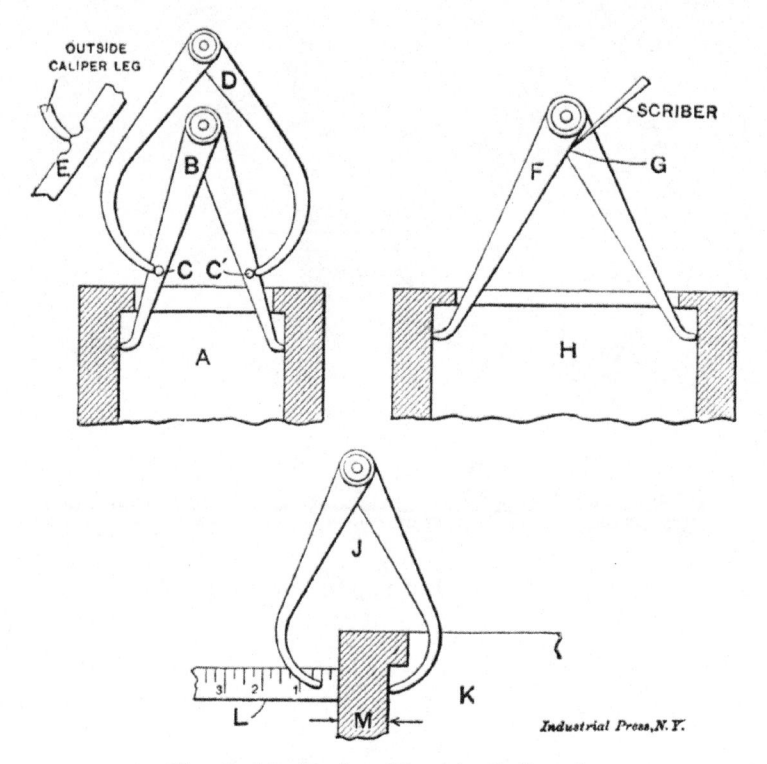

Fig. 7. Methods of Inside Calipering

MEASURING TOOLS

To get the thickness of a wall beyond a shoulder, as at K, Fig. 7, set the caliper so that the legs will pass over the shoulder freely, and with a scale measure the distance between the outside leg and the outside of the piece. Then remove the caliper and measure the distance between the caliper points. The difference between these two distances will be the thickness M.

Inside Calipers for Close Spaces

In Fig. 8 are shown a pair of inside calipers which are bent so as to be well adapted for calipering distances difficult of access, such as the keyway in a shaft and hub which does not extend beyond the hub, as indicated. With the ordinary inside calipers, having straight legs, and which are commonly used for inside work, it is generally impossible to get the exact size, as the end which is held in the hand comes in contact with the shaft before both points come into the same vertical plane. The engraving plainly shows how calipers for this purpose are made, and how used. Any mechanic can easily bend a common pair to about the shape shown to accommodate this class of work.[3]

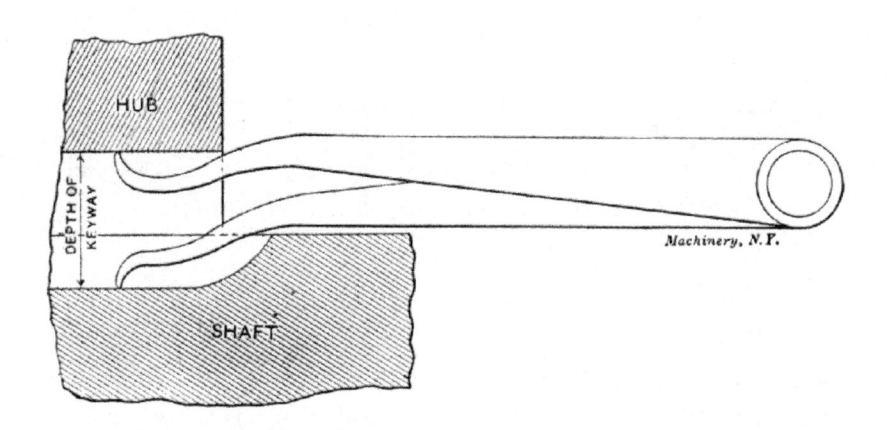

Fig. 8. Inside Calipers for Close Spaces

Surface Gage with Two Pointers

Figs. 9 and 10 show a special surface gage and illustrate an original idea which has been found to be a great saver of time and of milling cutters. It can also be used on the planer or shaper. By its use the operator can raise the milling machine table to the right height without testing the cut two or three times and eliminate the danger of taking a cut that is liable to break the cutter. This tool is especially valuable on castings, as raising the table and allowing the cutter to revolve in the gritty surface while finding the lowest spot is very disastrous to the cutting edges.

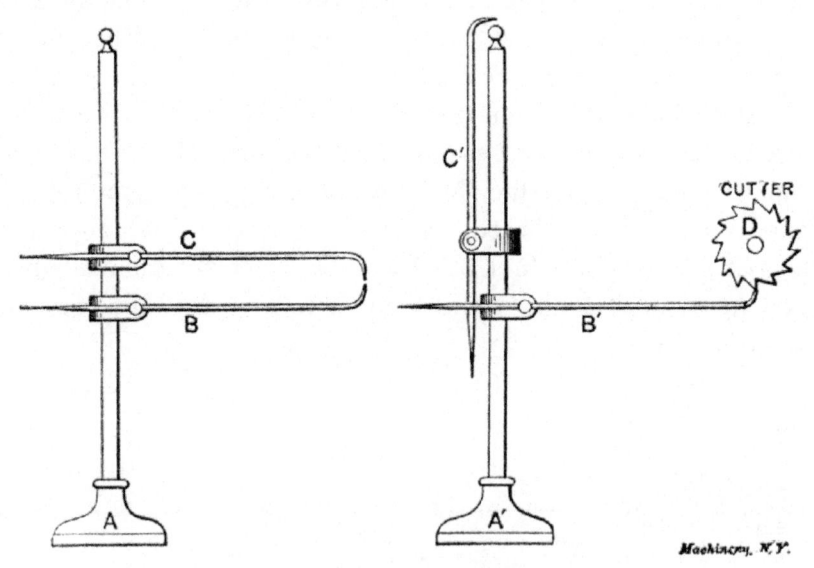

Figs. 9 and 10. Surface Gage with Two Pointers

To use this surface gage, the pointer marked C in Fig. 9 is set to the lowest spot in the casting, and then the pointer B is set from it with perhaps 1/32 inch between the points for a cut sufficient to clean up the surface. Pointer C is then folded up as shown at C' in Fig. 10, and the table is raised until the pointer B will just touch the underside of the cutter as shown at B' in Fig. 10. In this way the table is quickly adjusted to a cut that will clean the casting or other piece being machined, and with no cutting or trying whatever.[4]

MEASURING TOOLS

To Adjust the Needle of a Surface Gage

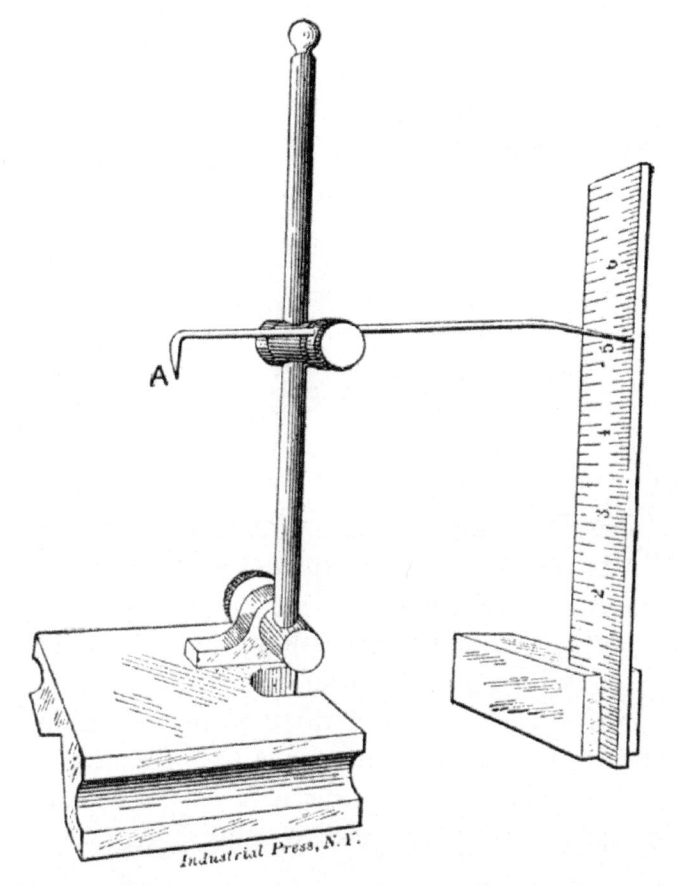

Fig. 11. Method of Adjusting the Needle of a Surface Gage

Fig. 11 illustrates a method of adjusting the needle of a surface gage. To set the gage 3¾ inches from the table, get somewhere within ¼ inch of the mark on the square. With the thumb and forefinger on hook A, turn the needle till it reaches the point desired. By turning the needle, it will travel in a circular path, on account of the bend near the point, and thus reach the desired setting.

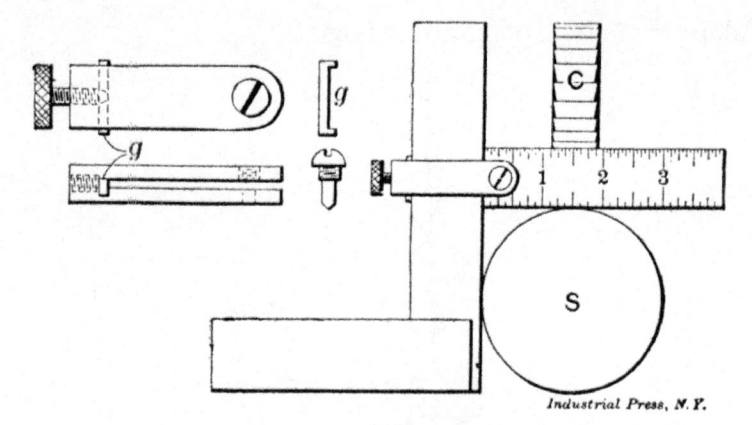

Fig. 12. Scale Attachment for the Square

Scale Attachment for the Square

Fig. 12 shows a device for attaching a scale to a square. This combination makes a very convenient tool to use when setting up work for keyseating, as is illustrated in the engraving, in which S is the shaft to be splined and C the milling cutter. It is also a very handy tool for truing up work on the boring mill or lathe. At the upper left-hand corner, is shown the construction of the parts, which are made of dimensions to suit the size of the scale and the square. For the combination to be successful, it is essential that the blade of the square is the same thickness as the scale.[5]

Attachment for Machinist's Scale

Fig. 13 shows a very convenient appliance. It will be found very useful in the machine shop for setting inside calipers to any desired size. The gage is clamped over the rule wherever desired, and one leg of the calipers set against the gage, the other leg being brought flush with the end of the scale.[6]

MEASURING TOOLS

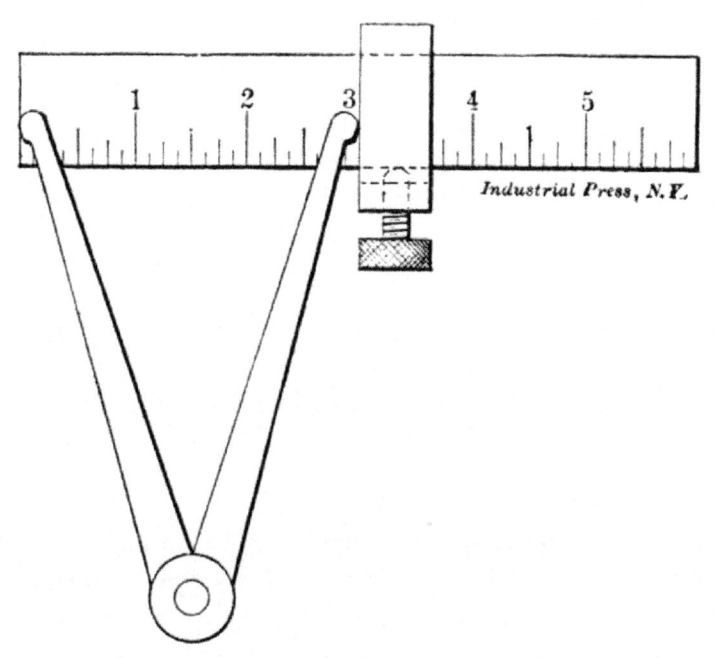

Fig. 13. Convenient Attachment for Machinist's Scale

Setting Dividers Accurately

To set dividers accurately, take a 1-inch micrometer and cut a line entirely around the thimble as at A, Fig. 14, and then, with the instrument set at zero, make a punch mark B exactly one inch from the line on the thimble. If less than one inch is wanted, open out the micrometer and set the dividers to the dot and line so as to give one inch more than the distance wanted. Now with the dividers make two marks across a line, as at a and b, Fig. 14, and then set the dividers to one inch and mark another line as at c. The distance from c to b is the amount desired, and the dividers can be set to it. Great care must, of course, be exercised, if accurate results are required.

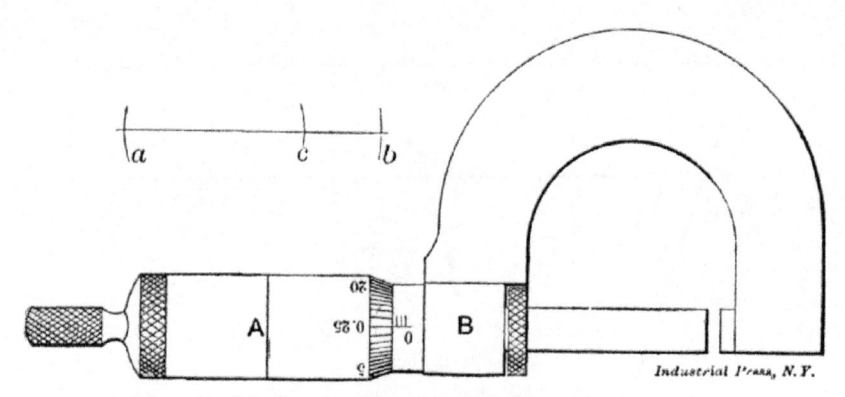

Fig. 14. Method of Setting Dividers Accurately

Combination Caliper and Divider

The combination caliper and divider shown in Fig. 15 is one that is not manufactured by any of the various tool companies. It is, however, one of the handiest tools that can be in a machinist's kit, as it lends itself to so many varied uses, and often is capable of being used where only a special tool can be employed. The illustration suggests its usefulness. The tool can be used as an outside caliper, as an inside caliper, and as a divider. The common form of this tool has generally only one toe on the caliper legs, but the double toes save the reversal of the points when changing from outside to inside work. The divider points may be set at an angle, which permits of stepping off readily around the outside of a shaft at angular distances, where the ordinary dividers are useless. A number of other uses could be mentioned, but any intelligent mechanic can readily suggest them for himself.

MEASURING TOOLS

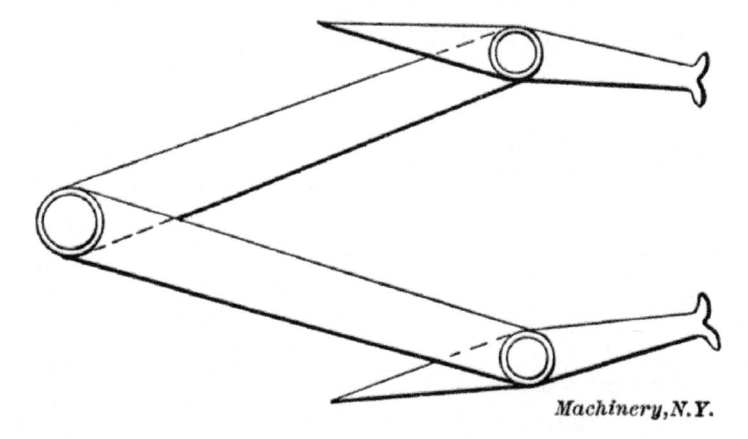

Fig. 15. Combination Caliper and Divider

Attachment for Vernier Calipers

While vernier and slide calipers are very handy shop tools, their usefulness is much more limited than it ought to be for such expensive instruments. In order to increase the usefulness of these tools, the attachments shown in Fig. 16 may be made. In the upper left-hand part of the engraving the details of a useful addition to the caliper are shown. A is made of machine steel, while the tongue B is of tool steel, hardened and ground and lapped to a thickness of 0.150 inch, the top and bottom being absolutely parallel. This tongue is secured to A by the two rivets CC. The thumb-screw D is used for fastening the attachment to the sliding jaw of the vernier or slide caliper. In the upper part of the engraving is shown the base, which is of machine steel, with the slot F milled for the reception of the fixed jaw of the caliper. The setscrews GGG are put in at a slight angle so that the caliper will be held firmly and squarely in this base. In the figure to the left these pieces are shown in the position for forming a height gage, for which purpose the attachment is most commonly used. As a test of the accuracy of its construction when the attachment is placed in this position, the tongue B should make a perfect joint with the fixed jaw of the caliper, and the vernier should give a reading of exactly 0.150. When it is desirable that the tongue B should overhang, the base E is pushed back even with the stationary jaw, as shown in the engraving to the right. In this position it is used for laying out and testing bushings in jigs, etc. The illustration shows the tool in use for this purpose, K being the jig to be tested. All measurements are from the center line upon which the bushing No. 1 is placed. Taking this as a starting point we find the caliper to read 1 inch. Bushing No. 2, which is undergoing the test, should be ⅝ inch from this center line. It has a ¼-inch hole, and we therefore insert a plug of this diameter. Now adjust the tongue of the caliper to the bottom of this plug (as shown in the engraving) and the vernier should read 1.625 minus one-half the diameter of the plug, or 1.500, and any variation from this will show the error of the jig. In this case the top surface of B was used, and no allowance had to be made for its thickness. In case the bottom surface is used, 0.150 must be deducted from the reading of the caliper.

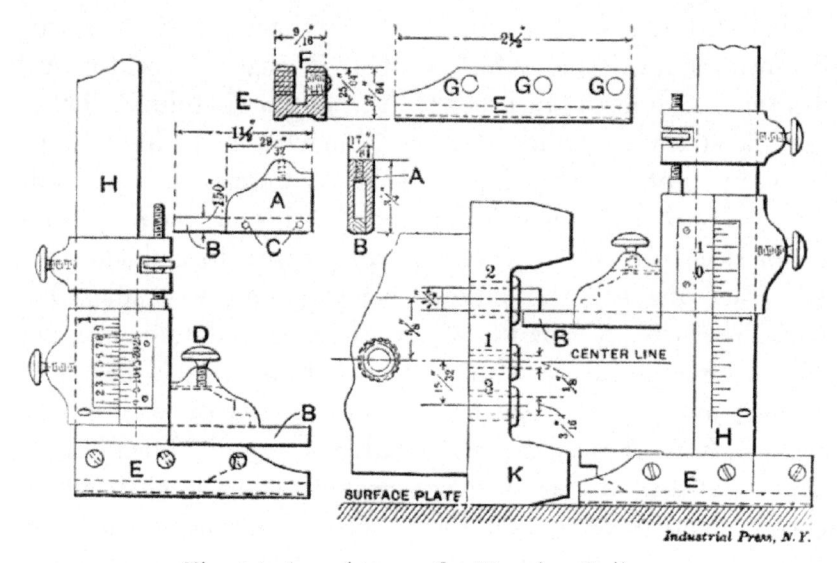

Fig. 16. Attachment for Vernier Calipers

It is very easy to make a mistake in setting a bushing, and such a mistake is equally hard to detect unless some such means of measuring as this is at hand. It often happens that jigs and fixtures are put into use containing such errors, and the trouble is not discovered until many dollars' worth of work has been finished and found worthless. The illustration shows but one of the many uses to which this attachment may be applied. The figures given on the details are correct for making an attachment to be used upon the Brown & Sharpe vernier caliper, but for other calipers they would, of course, have to be altered to suit.[7]

Improved Micrometer Beam Caliper

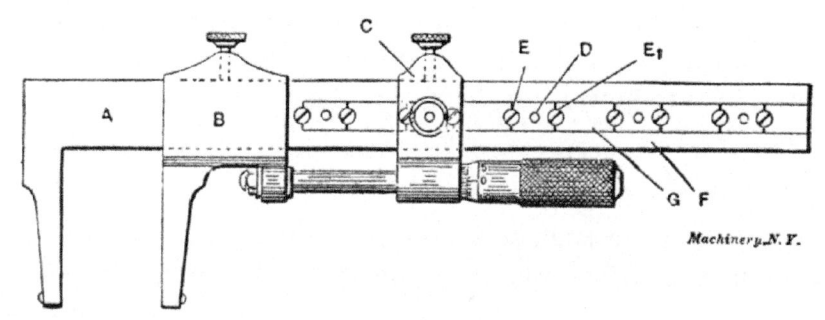

Fig. 17. Improved Micrometer Beam Caliper

In a beam caliper having a sliding micrometer jaw with or without a separate clamping slide, it is necessary to have the beam divided into unit spaces, at which the jaw or slide may be accurately fixed, the micrometer screw then being used to cover the distance between the divisions; but it is difficult to construct a beam caliper of this type with holes for a taper setting pin, at exactly equal distances apart; consequently a plan that is generally followed in making such tools is to provide as many holes through the slide and beam as there are inch divisions, each hole being drilled and reamed through both the slide and beam at once. If it were attempted to drill the holes through the beam at exactly one inch apart, having only one hole in the clamping head and using it as a jig for the purpose, it would be found very difficult, if not impossible, to get the holes all of one size and exactly one inch apart. The design of the micrometer beam caliper shown in Fig. 17, which has been patented by Mr. Frank Spalding, Providence, Rhode Island, is such, however, that it is not necessary to drill more than one hole through the clamping slide. The beam F is grooved longitudinally, and in the groove are fitted hardened steel adjusting blocks in which a taper hole D is accurately finished. Between the blocks are filling pieces G, which are brazed or otherwise fastened in the groove. Holes are drilled, tapped, and countersunk between the blocks and the filling pieces G, in which are fitted taper head screws EE_1. The construction is thus obviously such that the blocks may be shifted longitudinally by loosening one screw and tightening the other. In constructing the caliper, the holes through the beam are drilled as accurately as possible, one inch apart, and centered in the longitudinal groove, but are made larger than the holes in the blocks, so as to provide for slight adjustment.

Large Beam Caliper

Fig. 18 shows a large beam caliper designed for machinists and patternmakers. It consists of a beam MN and the legs R and S, made of cherry wood to the dimensions indicated. The legs are secured in position on the beam by means of the thumb screws A, which jam against the gibs C at the points of the screws. The gibs have holes countersunk for the screws to enter, to hold them approximately in place, and the nuts B are of brass, fitted into the filling pieces P that keep them from turning. The filling pieces are riveted to the legs by means of cherry dowels D. One leg S is provided with a fine adjustment consisting of flexible steel spring H, ending in a point which is adjusted by the thumb screw E. This screw is locked in adjustment by the check nut G bearing against the brass nut F, which is inserted in the leg as shown.[8]

MEASURING TOOLS

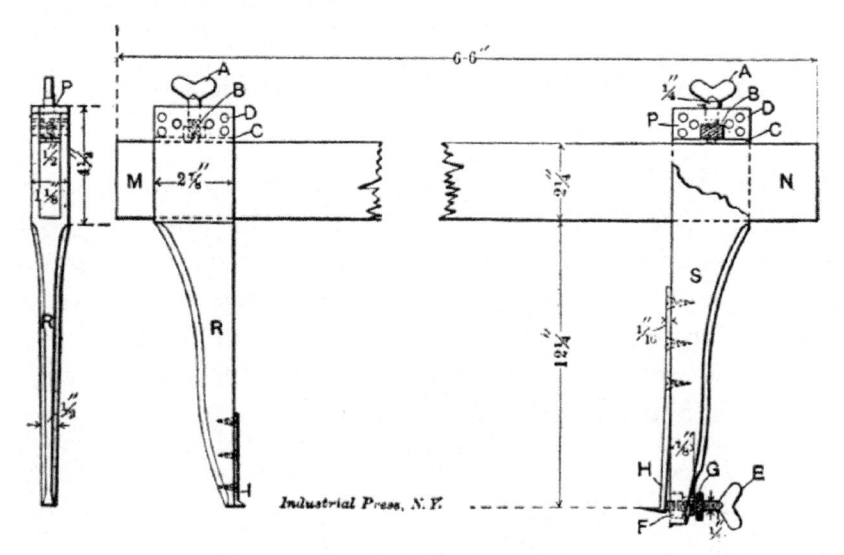

Fig. 18. Large Beam Caliper

CHAPTER III
MICROMETER MEASURING INSTRUMENTS

Of all measuring instruments used in the shop intended for accurate measurements, those working on the principle of the ordinary micrometer calipers are the most common. In the present chapter we shall describe and illustrate a number of different designs of these tools, intended to be used for various purposes. The instruments shown in Figs. 19 to 23 were built, in leisure hours, by Mr. A. L. Monrad, of East Hartford, Conn.

Micrometer for Snap Gages

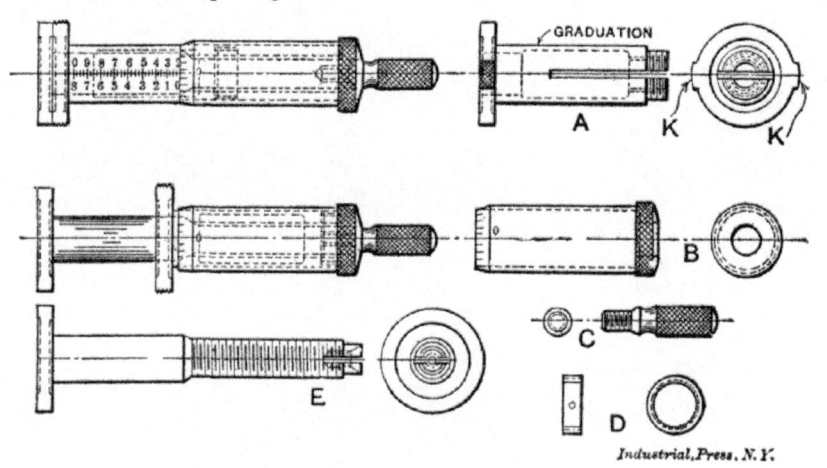

Fig. 19. Micrometer for Snap Gages

Fig. 19 shows a form of micrometer that has proved very handy for measuring snap gages, and thicknesses, and can also be used as a small height gage to measure the distance from a shoulder to the base, as shown in Fig. 20. In measuring snap gages or thicknesses, the outside and inside of the measuring disks are used, respectively. This instrument may also come in very handy when setting tools on the planer or shaper. As will be seen in the engraving, there are two sets of graduations on the sleeve A, thus enabling the operator to tell at a glance what measurement is obtained from the outside or

MEASURING TOOLS

the inside of the measuring disks. Each of the disks is 0.100-inch-thick, so that the range of the micrometer is 0.800 and 1.000 inch for the outside and inside, respectively. The details of the instrument are as follows:

The sleeve A is composed of the inside measuring disk, the graduated sleeve, and the micrometer nut combined. On the disk are two projections KK, which are knurled, thus providing a grip when operating the tool.

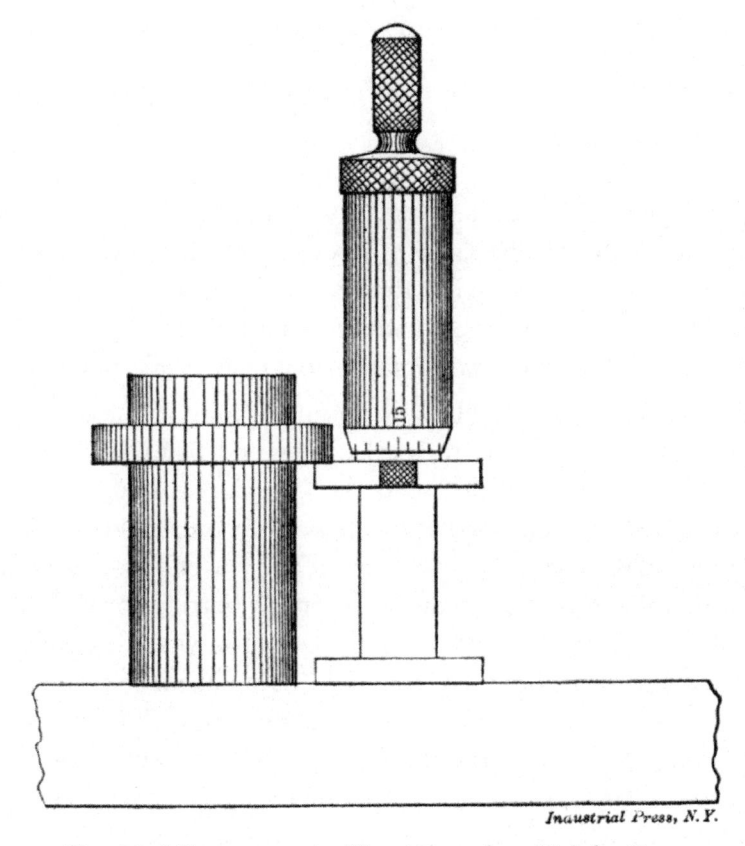

Fig. 20. Micrometer in Fig. 19 used as Height Gage

The sleeve is threaded on the inside of one end, which acts as a micrometer nut, and the outside of this same end is threaded to receive the adjusting nut D. The sleeve has two slots, each placed 90 degrees from the graduations, and these provide for compensation for wear. The disk part is hardened by heating in a lead bath and is finished by grinding and lapping. The barrel B is the same as a regular micrometer barrel and is graduated with 25 divisions. Spindle E consists of the outside disk and the micrometer screw, and the barrel B fits on its end, which is tapped out to receive the speeder C, which serves to hold the barrel in position. The thread is ¼ inch, 40 pitch, and the disk and unthreaded parts are hardened, ground and lapped. To adjust this, instrument, loosen the speeder C and turn the barrel until the proper adjustment is obtained. Then lock the barrel by tightening the speeder again.[9]

Micrometer Caliper Square

Fig. 21 shows an assembled view and the details of a micrometer caliper square which, if accurately made, is equal and often preferable to the vernier caliper now so generally used. One of its advantages over the vernier is that when the measurement is taken, it can be readily discerned without straining the eyes, and this instrument is as easy to manipulate as the regular micrometer.

In the details, part A, which is the main body of the instrument, is made of tool steel, the forward or jaw end being solid with the body. This end is hardened, and the jaw ground and lapped. The body is bored out and two flats milled on the outside, which lighten it up and make it neat in appearance. The jaw end is counterbored out with a 45-degree counterbore to form a bearing for the forward end of the micrometer screw. A slot, ⅛ inch in width, extends from the fixed jaw to the other end, and in this slides the movable jaw C. There are 44 divisions along the side of this slot, each division being 0.050 inch apart, giving the tool a range of 2.000 inches for outside and 2.200 inches for inside measurements. The screw B is the most essential part of this tool, its construction requiring great accuracy. Its diameter is ⅜ inch and it is cut with 20 threads per inch. On its forward end fits the cone F, which is hardened and ground, the round part acting as the forward bearing of the screw and fitting in the 45-degree counterbored hole in the body A. On its other end fits the graduated barrel D and also the speeder G.

MEASURING TOOLS

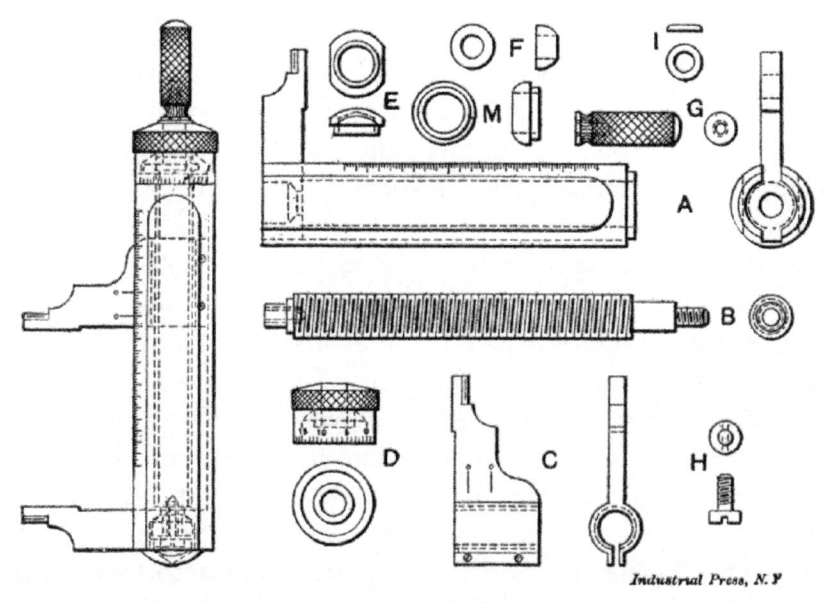

Fig. 21. Micrometer Caliper Square

The barrel is graduated in fifty divisions, each division equaling 0.001 inch. On the inside of the barrel is a 45-degree bearing which rides on the cone M, the cone being held stationary on the end of the body. Thus, it will be seen that both front and back ends of the micrometer screw are carried in cone bearings, which give a very small point of contact, thereby causing but little friction and preventing any danger of gumming up so as to run hard. The sliding jaw C is made of tool steel, hardened, ground and lapped, and combined with it is the micrometer nut which is drawn to a spring temper. This nut is split and adjusted by two screws to compensate for wear. On this jaw are the two zero marks that tell at a glance the outside or inside measurements taken. The screw and washer, marked H and I, go onto the end of the micrometer screw and take up the end play. To make a neat appearance, the cap E is placed in the forward counterbored hole, being held in place by a tight fit. The adjustment of the tool is accomplished by loosening the speeder G and turning the barrel on the screw; when the adjustment is made, the speeder is again tightened down and the barrel locked.[10]

Micrometer Depth Gage

The depth gage, shown in Fig. 22, has a ½-inch movement of the rod, and may be used with rods of any desired length. These have small 45-degree-on-a-side grooves cut into them at intervals of ½ inch. A small spiral spring, marked I, gives the rod a constant downward pressure, so that, when taking a measurement, the base of the tool is placed on the piece of work, and the rod always finds the bottom of the hole; then, by tightening the knurled screw F the rod is clamped in position and the tool may be picked up and its measurement read from the dial. The graduations on this instrument are similar to those of the vernier caliper, only they are much plainer, as a half-inch movement of the rod turns the dial one complete revolution. The figures on the dial denote tenths of an inch, and those on the body of the tool thousandths; each graduation on the dial is therefore equal to 0.010, so that to show the depth of a hole to be 0.373 the dial would be revolved around so that the seventh division beyond the 3 mark would be near to 0, and then by looking from the 0 mark toward the left, the third graduation on the body and one on the dial would be in line, thus denoting 0.373.

The most essential part of this tool is the threaded screw B, which acts as a rack, and the worm-wheel, solid with the dial C. The upper end of the screw forms a split chuck which grips the measuring rods, while the part marked R is flatted off, and against this portion bears a threaded sleeve G, which acts as a key to keep the screw in position. This sleeve is threaded, both inside and outside, and screws into the body of the tool, while the binding screw F fits into it and binds against a small piece of copper, marked H, which in turn holds the screw in position. The thread on B is 0.245 inch in diameter and is cut with 40 threads per inch. The worm-wheel which meshes into this screw is solid with the dial, as shown at C. It is 0.18 inch in diameter and requires great accuracy in cutting; it is not hobbed, but the teeth, of which there are twenty, are milled with a circular cutter of the same diameter as the screw B plus 0.002 inch. The little studs, marked EE, on the dial and on the body K, hold the coiled spring in position. Very great accuracy must be attained when locating the holes in K that are to receive the screw and dial B and C. The screw marked J fits into the dial, where it serves as a bearing and also holds the dial in position. The knurled cap D tightens the split chuck in order to hold the measuring rod firmly.[11]

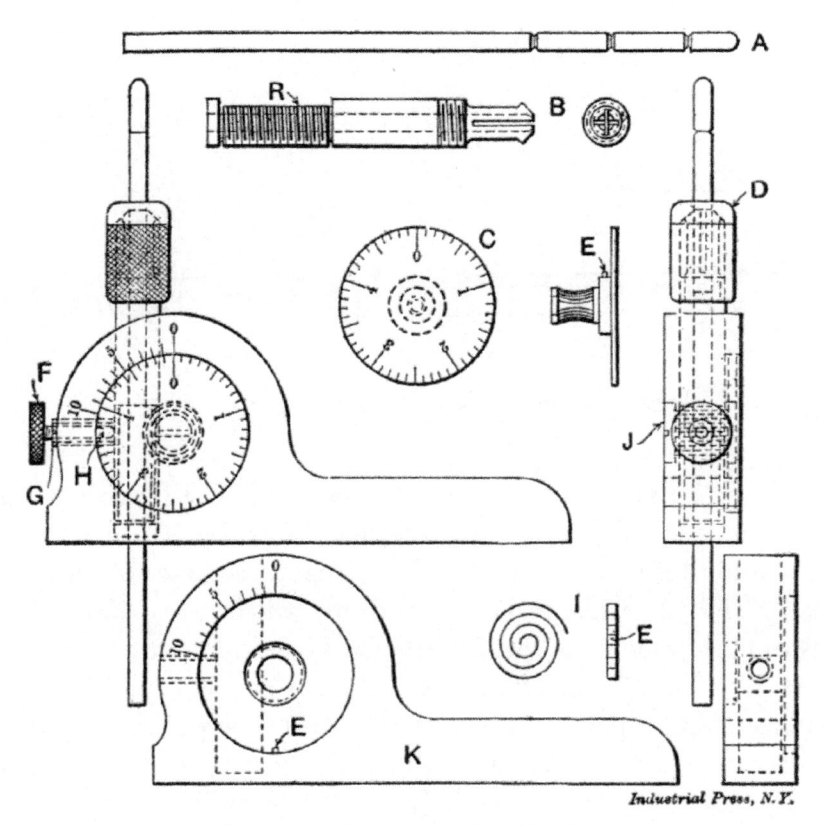

Fig. 22. Micrometer Depth Gage

MD. ANAMUL HASAN

Indicator for Accuracy of Leadscrews

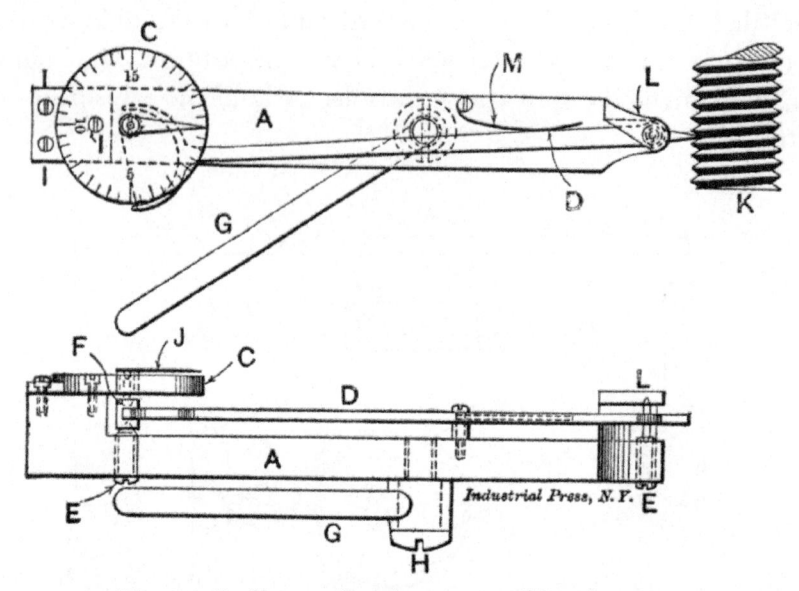

Fig. 23. Indicator for Accuracy of Leadscrews

All of the tools that have been described require an accurately cut screw, and, as very few lathes are capable of producing this, it may be well to illustrate an indicator for testing the accuracy of the leadscrew, and to explain the method by which it is used. This instrument is shown in Fig. 23, where it is applied to a test screw K. It consists of a body A on one end of which is a projection L serving as the upper bearing for the pivoted lever D. This lever swings about a small steel pivot which can be adjusted by the screw E. The rear end of the lever is forked, and between the prongs is passed a thread making a double turn about the pivot F that carries the pointer J. Any movement of this lever will, therefore, cause this pointer to revolve about the dial C. This dial has 20 divisions, each indicating one-half thousandth of an inch movement of the front end of the lever, so that a total revolution of the pointer about the dial would indicate a movement of the front end of the lever of 0.020 inch. The screws I serve to hold the dial in place on the body of the indicator, while the spring M keeps the pointer normally at

MEASURING TOOLS

the zero mark. The indicator is held in the toolpost by the arm G, which can be set at any angle and firmly clamped by the screw H.

To use the indicator, remove the screw from a micrometer which is known to be accurate, and, with the aid of a brass bushing, chuck it in the lathe so that the thread end will project. Now gear the lathe to cut 40 threads per inch and apply the indicator. When the lathe is started, the point of the indicator follows along in the thread of the micrometer screw, and any variation in the lead will be noted by a movement of the pointer over the dial. If, on the other hand, no movement takes place, it is an indication that the pitch of the lead-screw is correct.[12]

Micrometer Attachment for Reading Ten-thousandths of an Inch

Fig. 24 shows an attachment for micrometers designed and made for readings in tenths of thousandths of an inch. With very little fitting it is interchangeable for 1-, 2-, or 3-inch B. & S. micrometers. The idea is simple, as can be seen by the illustration. The diameter of the thimble is increased 3 to 1 by a disk which is graduated with 250 lines instead of 25, making each line represent 0.0001 inch instead of 0.001 inch.

Fig. 24. Micrometer with Attachment for Reading Ten-thousandths of an Inch

A piece of steel is then turned up and bored and cut away so as to form the index blade and a shell to clasp the micrometer frame, the whole thing being made in one piece. The thimble disk being just a good wringing fit, it can be easily adjusted 0 to 0. The attachment can be removed when fine measuring is not required.[13]

Special Micrometer for Large Dimensions

Fig. 25 shows a 6-inch micrometer caliper designed for measuring from 0 to 6 inches by half-thousandths. The sliding micrometer head travels on a cylinder barrel through which a hole is accurately bored to suit three plugs, one, two, and three inches long, as shown in the engraving. These plugs serve to locate the traveling head at fixed distances one inch apart. The micrometer screw itself has a travel of one inch, like any standard micrometer. A locknut is used to hold the screw in any desired position. A thumb screw at the end of the barrel bears against the end plug, and zero marks are provided to bring the screw against the plug with the same degree of pressure at each setting. When the head is clamped by means of the locking nut, it is as rigid as though it were solid with the barrel, and the faces of the measuring points are thus always parallel.

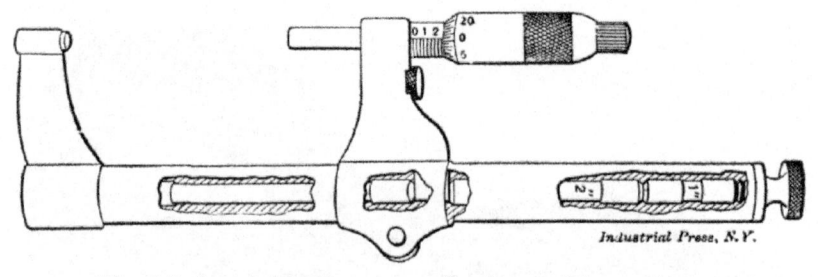

Fig. 25. Special Micrometer for Large Dimensions

MEASURING TOOLS

Combination Micrometer

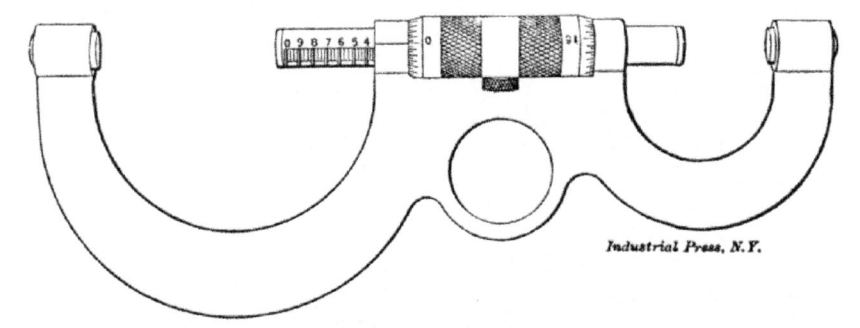

Fig. 26. Combined One- and Two-inch Micrometer

A combined one- and two-inch micrometer is shown in Fig. 26. One side records measurements up to one inch, and the other side up to two inches. A single knurled sleeve or nut serves to move the double-ended measuring piece one way or the other as desired, this piece having a travel of one inch. The spindle is non-rotating, so that the faces of the screw and anvil are always parallel. A locking device holds the screw in any position. This tool is convenient for use both in measuring and as a gage, since it can be conveniently held by the finger ring appearing at the back.

Micrometer Stop for the Lathe

Most micrometer lathe stops are limited in their use to work where only a stationary height is required. It is, however, often necessary to use the stop at different heights, to accommodate different lathes; then again, we wish to use it on the right-hand side as well as the left. The form of holder shown in Fig. 27 can be used either right or left, and for various heights, and, by simply taking out the screw A, the micrometer may be removed and used in any other form of holder desired.

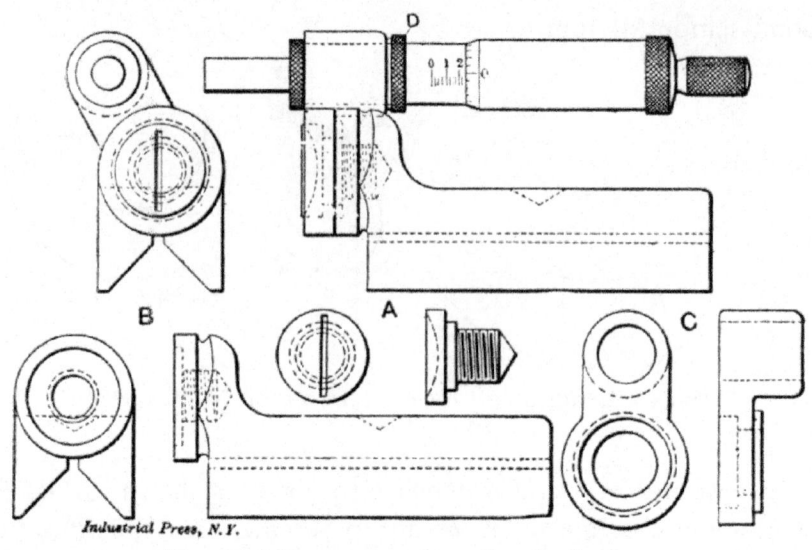

Fig. 27. Micrometer Stop for the Lathe

Both an assembled view and details of the holder are shown in the engraving, so that it can be easily constructed by anyone desiring to do so. The micrometer and barrel may be procured from any of the manufacturers of measuring instruments. The swivel C is bored out so that the axis of the micrometer screw will be parallel to the body of the holder when it is in place. The swivel is made of tool steel and is fastened to the holder by the screw A. It is hardened and lapped to a true bearing surface on the sides and bottom, and so adjusted that it will turn to either side and remain in the desired position without moving the screw. The holder B is milled through its entire length with a 90-degree cutter so that it will fit along the ways of the lathe, and the bottom is lapped to a true surface. For a neat appearance, the tool should be color hardened. On top the holder is spotted or countersunk with a drill to form a recess for the C-clamp. A knurled ring D is driven onto the micrometer sleeve so that it can be turned around to bring the graduations uppermost when the position of the barrel is changed.[14]

Micrometer Surface and Height Gage

Fig. 28 shows a form of surface gage that has proved very handy, and which can be used also as a height gage for measuring distances from shoulders to the base. If accurately made it is equal, and often preferable, to the vernier or slide caliper now so generally used with an attachment to the sliding jaw. One of its advantages over the vernier is the readiness with which the graduations are discerned, and it is as easy to manipulate as the ordinary micrometer. The part B, which forms the main body of the instrument, is made of tool steel, and one end is fitted into the base where it is held in position by the screw D. The remainder is milled to a thickness of ⅛ inch and has graduations of 0.025 inch for a distance of three inches. The screw A is the most essential part of the tool, and its construction requires great accuracy. Its diameter is ½ inch, and it is cut with 20 threads per inch. In the upper end of the screw is driven the ball H for the sake of giving a neat appearance. The top of the thread is turned off 0.010 inch to allow the scriber F to slide freely on the screw. The barrel I is used for raising and lowering the slide, but instead of having the graduations placed directly upon it, they are made upon the sleeve C, which fits over a shoulder on the barrel. This allows easier means of adjustment than would be possible were the graduations placed on the barrel itself. The sleeve is graduated with fifty divisions each equaling a movement of the scriber of 0.001 inch. This sleeve may be turned by means of a small spanner wrench so as to bring the zero line into correct position to compensate for wear. A knurled locking nut is also provided for holding the scriber in any fixed position.

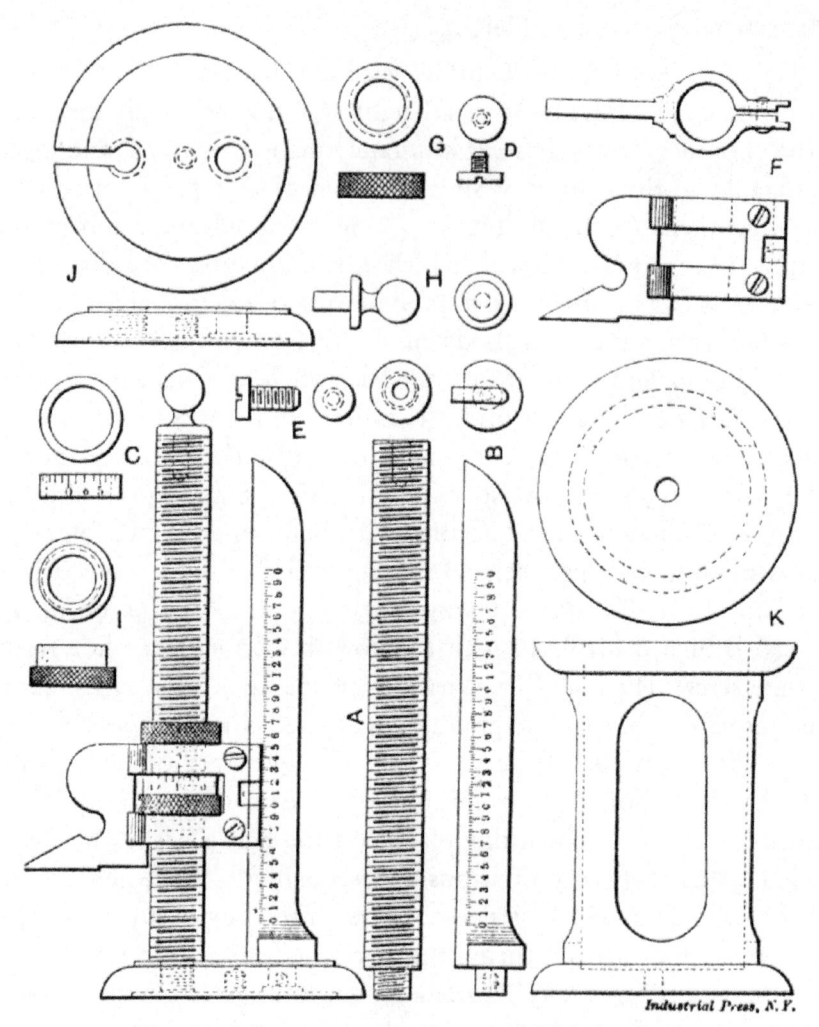

Fig. 28. Micrometer Surface and Height Gage

    The scriber itself is hardened and lapped to a finished surface, the tail end being slotted and provided with two screws to compensate for wear. On the scriber is placed the zero mark which shows at a glance the measurement that is being taken. The block K is three inches in height, and by using this block and placing the gage on its top, the range of the gage is increased to six inches. The screw E is used for fastening the gage to the top of the block. The center of the block is drilled out and slots cut through the sides in order to make it light and neat in appearance.[15]

Micrometer of from One- to Five-inch Capacity

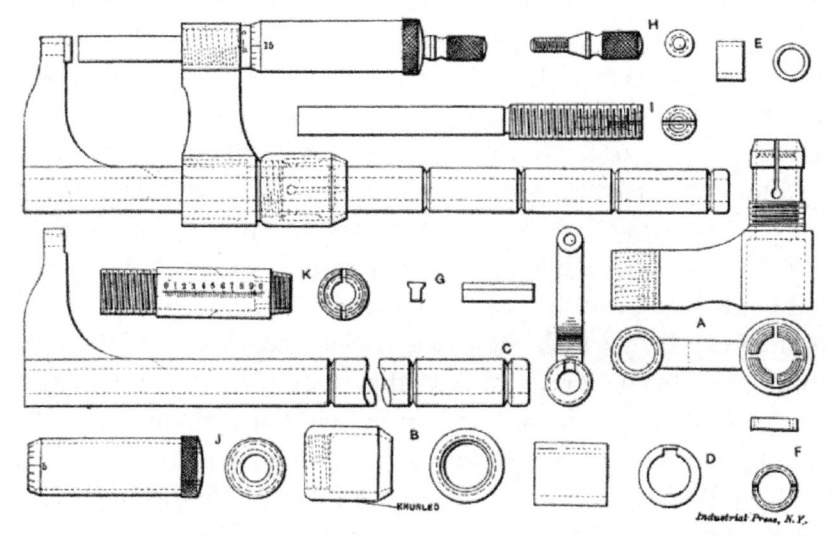

Fig. 29. Micrometer of from One- to Five-inch Capacity

Fig. 29 shows a very simple and light five-inch micrometer that can be quickly set to exact position from one to five inches. The round beam is graduated by a series of angular grooves, 1 inch apart, which are of such a form and depth that the clamping fingers at the end of part A spring in, allowing one-inch adjustment of the beam to be quickly and positively made. The sleeve K is of tool steel, being counterbored from the forward end for all but one-half inch of its length. For this half inch it is threaded on the inside and acts as a micrometer nut. The outside of the same end is threaded to receive the adjusting nut F, and two slots are cut in the sleeve, at 90 degrees with the graduations. These slots, by a movement of the nut F, provide a means for compensating for wear. The bushing E is hardened and lapped and fitted tightly in the forward counterbore of this sleeve, where it acts as a guide for the front end of the micrometer screw. The barrel J is the same as that of a regular micrometer and is graduated in 0.025-inch divisions.

The most essential part of the tool is the threaded screw I, over the end of which fits the barrel J. The end is tapped out to receive the speeder H, which serves to hold the barrel in position. The thread is 5/16 inch in diameter, with 40 threads per inch, while the unthreaded part is hardened, ground and lapped. To adjust the instrument, loosen the speeder H and turn the barrel until the proper adjustment is obtained; lock the barrel by again tightening the speeder. The beam C has a ¼-inch hole drilled throughout its entire length in order to make it light. Small 90-degree grooves are cut into it at intervals of 1 inch, and a ⅛-inch slot is milled through one side to within 1¼ inch of the forward end. The back end of part A forms a spring-tempered split chuck, which grips the beam and holds A in position, while the exterior is threaded to receive the knurled cap B by which the chuck is tightened firmly to the beam. From the front end, toward the split chuck, the body is counterbored ⅝ inch and the bushing D driven in tight. This bushing has a key G fitted into it, which slides in the slot of the beam and prevents the arm from turning. The projecting arm is bored and tapped to receive the sleeve K. This gage must be carefully and accurately made to be of value.[16]

Inside Micrometer for Setting Calipers

Fig. 30 shows an application of inside micrometers which is very handy. The hole for the scriber in the scriber clamp of a surface gage is reamed out to fit the rods used with inside micrometers. This forms a convenient holder for the micrometer when used for setting outside calipers to it. The calipers can be set easily and accurately at the same time, and where extreme accuracy is not necessary this arrangement is handier than that of using large-sized micrometers.

MEASURING TOOLS

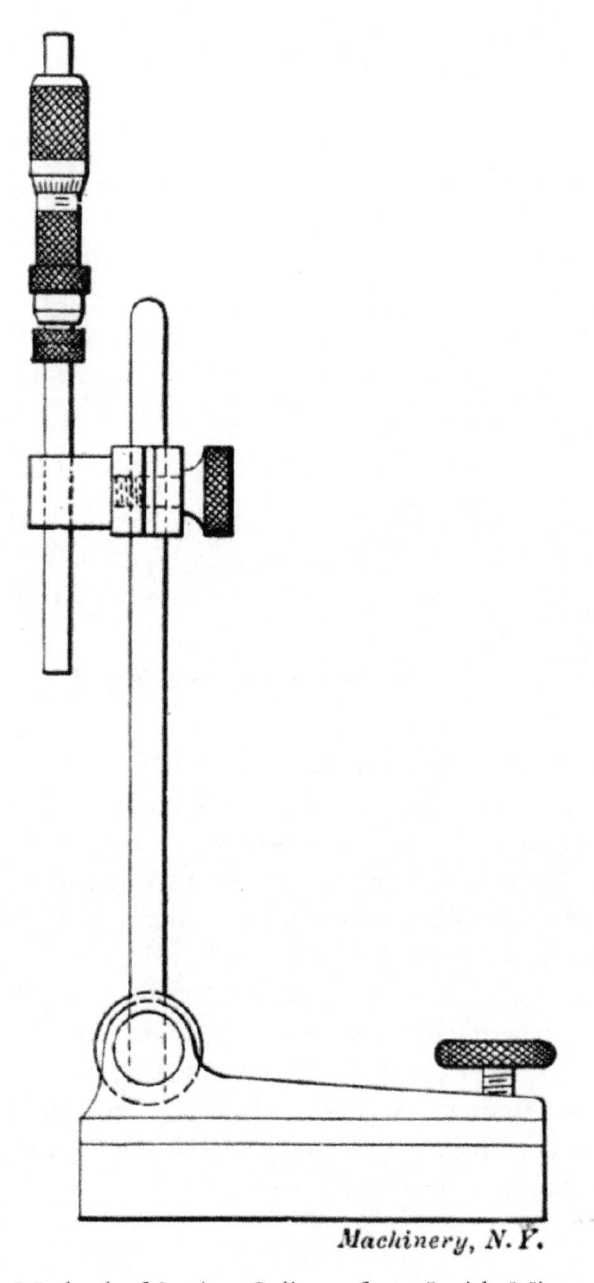

Fig. 30. Method of Setting Calipers from Inside Micrometers

With care and practice an accuracy of within one-quarter of 0.001 inch is obtainable in this way. Mistakes, in fact, are more easily guarded against than is the case when using the micrometers directly.

Micrometer Frame

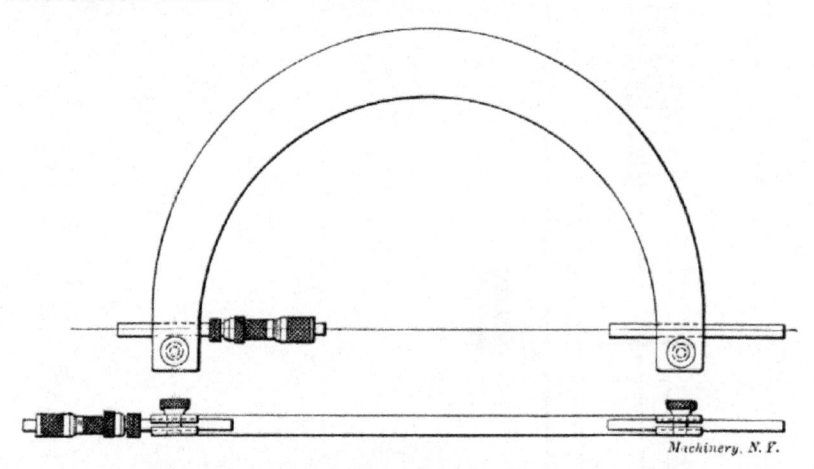

Fig. 31. Useful and Handy Micrometer Frame

Fig. 31 shows a micrometer frame used some years ago at the Westinghouse works. The frame is an aluminum casting, and the anvil is simply a tool-steel pin, which fits well in the hole into which it is inserted and can be clamped anywhere within the limits of its length. The micrometer end of the frame is supplied with an inside micrometer head. The tool is adjusted to a gage, either to a standard pin gage, or to an inside micrometer gage. The capacities of three of these micrometers in a set may be from about $3\frac{1}{2}$ to 7 inches, 6 to 11 inches, and 10 to 15 inches. When the head is turned outward, as shown in the lower view in the cut, the tool is very handy around a horizontal boring machine where a pin gage cannot be used without removing the boring bar.

MEASURING TOOLS

Micrometer Stop for the Lathe

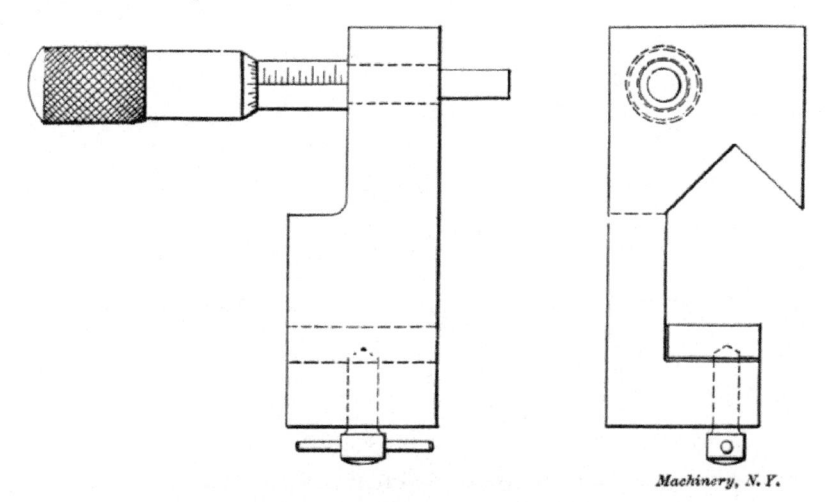

Machinery, N.Y.

Fig. 32. Micrometer Stop for the Lathe

The simple micrometer stop shown in Fig. 32 is used on the engine lathe for obtaining accurate movements of the lathe carriage. It consists of a micrometer head, which can be purchased from any micrometer manufacturer, and a machine steel body which is bored to fit the micrometer head. This tool is clamped on the front way of the lathe bed, and when the jaw of the micrometer is against the lathe carriage, it can easily be adjusted to a thousandth of an inch. Of course, care should be taken not to bump the carriage against the micrometer.[17]

Use of Micrometer for Internal Thread Cutting

Fig. 33 illustrates a means of determining the size of internally threaded work. The work shown is intended for a lathe chuck. The outside diameter of the hub on the work is turned to the same size as the hubs on small faceplates which are furnished with all new lathes. The threaded size is then taken and transferred with a micrometer, over the anvil of which is fitted a 60-degree point as shown enlarged at A. In connection with a graduated cross-feed screw this greatly facilitates the work over the usual cut-and-try method.[18]

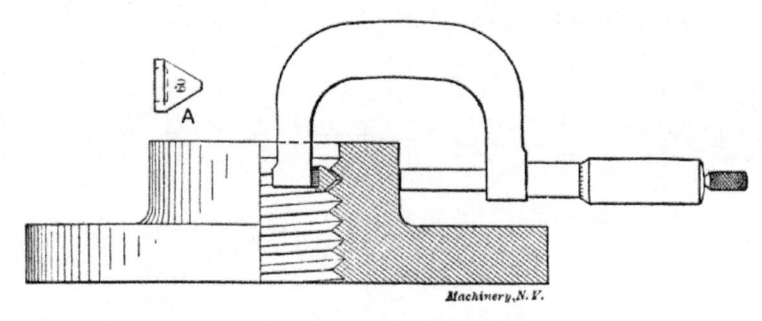

Fig. 33. Method of using Micrometer for Internal Thread Cutting

Inside Micrometer

The inside micrometer shown in sections in Figs. 34 and 35 is adapted to measuring, by use of extension rods, from 2 inches up to any size of hole, and has one-inch adjustment of the measuring screw.

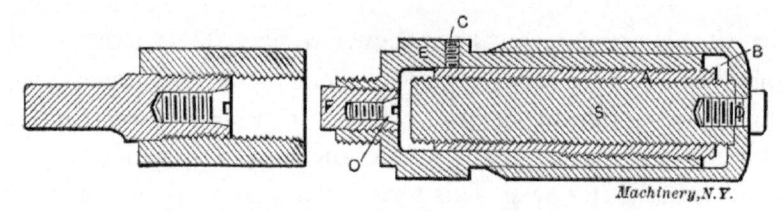

Figs. 34 and 35. Section of Inside Micrometer

Referring to the section shown in Fig. 35, the measuring screw S is secured to the thimble B with the screw D, the head of which is hardened and forms the anvil. By loosening this screw D, the thimble can be rotated to compensate for wear. The wear of the measuring screw and nut is taken up by screwing the bushing A into the frame with the wrench shown in Fig. 37. This bushing is split in three sections for about two-thirds of its length on the threaded end. The three small lugs on the wrench fit into these slots. The handle end of the wrench is a screwdriver which is used for manipulating the set screw C. The bushing is made an easy fit in the frame on its plain end and tapered, as shown, on its outside threaded part. This thread being the same pitch as the measuring screw, adjustment for wear does not affect the reading of the micrometer. This manner of adjustment brings the nut squarely down on the measuring screw for its whole length, presenting the same amount of wearing surface after adjustment as when new.

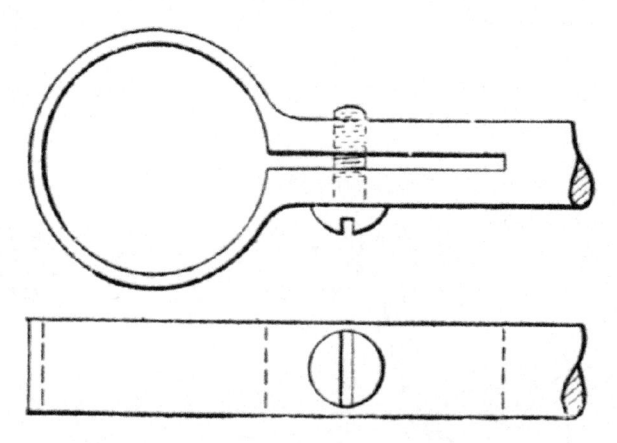

Fig. 36. Handle for Inside Micrometer

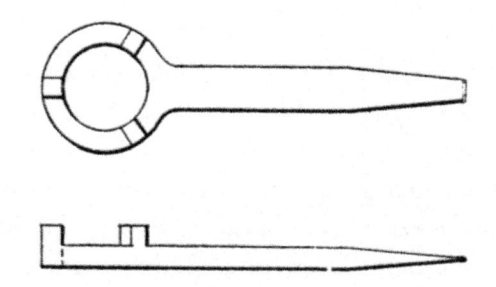

Fig. 37. Wrench used with Inside Micrometer

The point F, which is hardened on its outer end, screws into the frame, and is secured by the taper-headed screw O, which screws into and expands the split and threaded end of the point F. The handle, Fig. 36, clamps over the knurled part of the frame for use in small, deep holes. The rods, six in number, running from 1 to 6 inches inclusive, are made by screwing a sleeve onto a rod with a hardened point and locking it with a taper-headed screw on its threaded and split end, the same as in the point F. The extension pieces, Fig. 38, are adjustable, on their socketed ends, in the same way, and run in lengths of 6, 12, 18 inches, etc.[19]

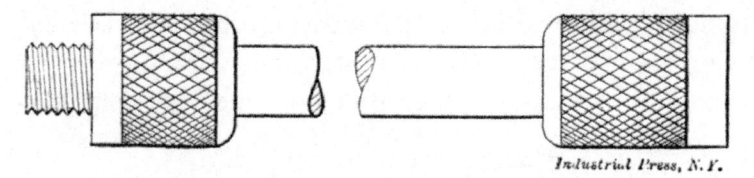

Fig. 38. Adjustable Extension Pieces for Inside Micrometer

Direct Fractional-reading Micrometer

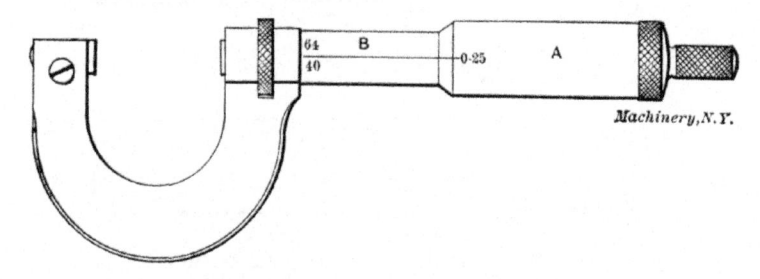

Fig. 39. Direct Fractional-reading Micrometer

The direct fractional-reading micrometer shown in Fig. 39 is the result of talks with many mechanics in which all agreed that such a feature added to a micrometer would, by making it both a fractional and decimal gage, more than double its practical value. While approximate readings in 64ths, etc., may be obtained by the graduations on the barrel B as on an ordinary inch scale, the exact readings of 64th, etc., may be obtained only by reference to graduations on the movable thimble A. There are but eight places on A which coincide with the long graduation line on B when any 64th, 32d, 16th, or 8th is being measured, and each of these eight places is marked with a line, and the 64th, 32d, 16th, or 8th for which that line should be used is marked thereon. (See a and b, Fig. 40.) The line a would be used for 3/32, 7/32, 11/32, etc., and the line b for 1/64, 9/64, 17/64, etc. Now suppose we wish to accurately measure 15/32 inch. We first roughly read it off the inch scale on sleeve B by turning out thimble A. Having secured it closely by drawing edge of A over that graduation, we find that the line a (Fig. 40) on the movable thimble very nearly or exactly coincides with the long graduation line on B. When these lines coincide, we have the exact measurement of 15/32 inch without reference to how many thousandths may be contained in the fraction. Thus, all through the scale any fraction may be found instantly. There is no mental arithmetic, use of tables, or memory work in using the tool. The new graduations are independent of the old and may be used equally well with or without them.

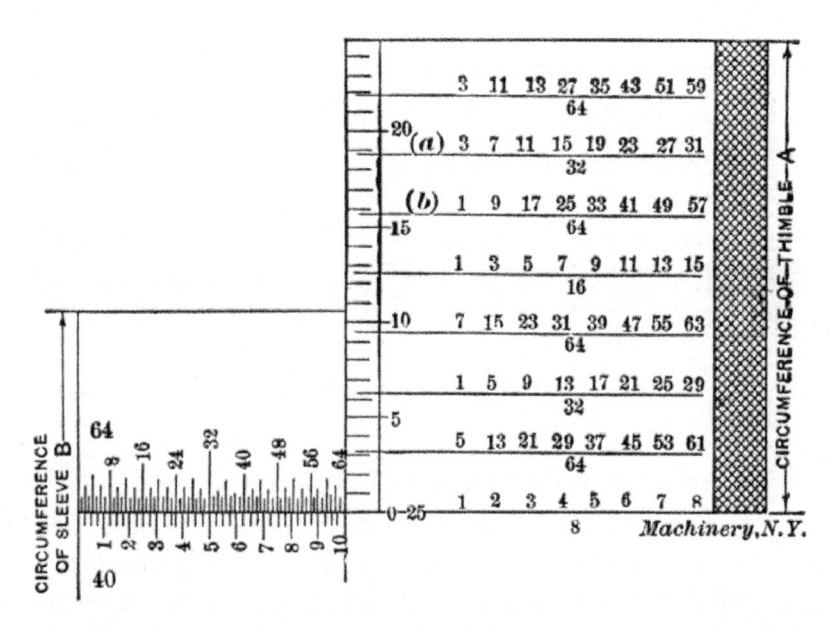

Fig. 40. Graduations on the Fractional-reading Micrometer

Micrometers may also be graduated as in Fig. 41. Instead of using the zero line on A as a base line, a point is taken one-fifth of a turnaround A, and the graduated scale on B is placed to correspond, as shown in the engraving; also, instead of making lines a, b, etc., on A, full length, they are made about half an inch long, and the numerators are entirely omitted and the denominators placed at the end instead of under the line. To the ordinary user of the tool, this is all that is necessary for a perfectly clear reading of the fractions.[20]

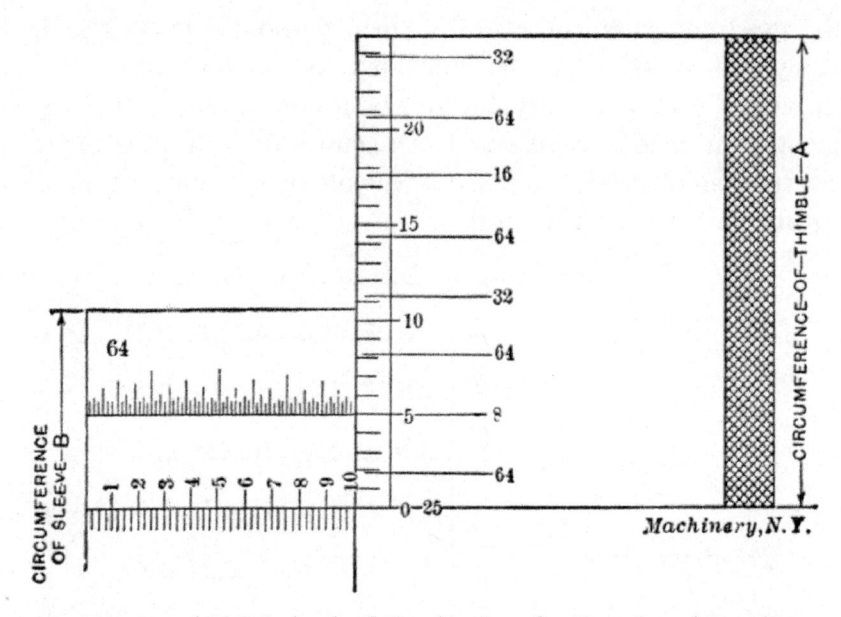

Fig. 41. Another Method of Graduating for Fractional Reading

Sensitive Attachment for Measuring Instruments

No matter how finely and accurately micrometers and verniers may be made, dependence must in all cases be placed on the sensitiveness of a man's hand to obtain the exact dimensions of the piece to be measured. In order to overcome this difficulty and eliminate the personal equation in the manufacture of duplicate and interchangeable parts, the sensitive attachment to the micrometer shown in Fig. 42 may be used and will be found of much value.

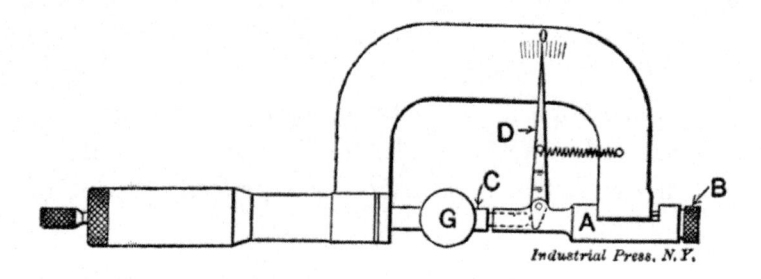

Fig. 42. Sensitive Micrometer Attachment

MEASURING TOOLS

The auxiliary barrel A is held to the anvil of the micrometer by means of a thumb screw B. At the inside end of the barrel is a secondary anvil C, the base of which bears against the short arm of the indicating lever D. The action will be clearly seen by reference to the engraving. The micrometer is so set that when a gage, G, of exact size, is placed between the measuring points, the long arm of the indicator stands at the 0 mark. If the pieces being calipered vary in the least from the standard size it will be readily noted by the movement of the pointer. Hard rubber shapes turned from rough casting often vary from 0.003 to 0.005 inch after having passed the inspector's test with an ordinary micrometer. With this attachment the inspector's helper can detect very minute variations from the limit size. Anything within the limits of the micrometer can be made to show to the naked eye variations as small as a ten-thousandth inch.[21]

Another Sensitive Micrometer Attachment

When testing the diameters of pieces that are handled in great quantities and are all supposed to be within certain close limits of a standard dimension, the ordinary micrometer presents the difficulty of having to be moved for each piece, and small variations in diameters have to be carefully read off from the graduations on the barrel. Not only does this take a comparatively long time, but it also easily happens that the differences from the standard diameter are not carefully noted, and pieces are liable to pass inspection that would not pass if a convenient arrangement for reading off the differences were at hand. Fig. 43 shows a regular Brown & Sharpe micrometer fitted with a sensitive arrangement for testing and inspecting the diameters of pieces which must be within certain close limits of variation. The addition to the ordinary micrometer is all at the anvil end of the instrument.

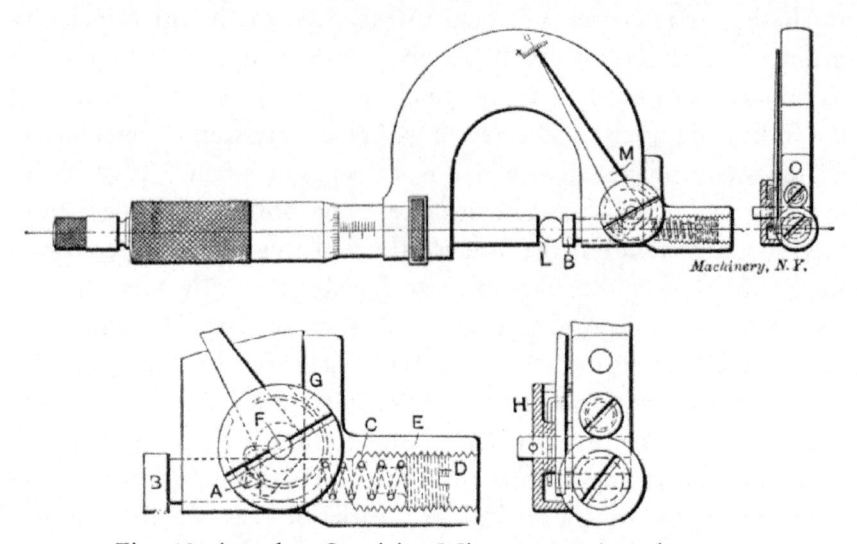

Fig. 43. Another Sensitive Micrometer Attachment

The anvil itself is loose and consists of a plunger B, held in place by a small pin A. The pin has freedom to move in a slot in the micrometer body, as shown in the enlarged view in the cut. A spring C holds the plunger B up against the work to be measured, and a screw D is provided for obtaining the proper tension in the spring. The screw and the spring are contained in an extension E screwed and doweled to the body of the micrometer. A pointer or indicator is provided which is pivoted at F and has one extensional arm resting against the pin A, which is pointed in order to secure a line contact. At the end of the indicator a small scale is graduated with the zero mark in the center, and as the indicator swings to one side or the other the variations in the size of the piece measured are easily determined. A small spring G is provided for holding the pointer up against the pin A. The case H simply serves the purpose of protecting the spring mentioned. As the plunger B takes up more space than the regular anvil, the readings of the micrometer cannot be direct. The plunger B can be made of such dimensions, however, that 0.100 inch deducted from the barrel and thimble reading will give the actual dimension. Such a deduction is easily done in all cases. In other words, the reading of the micrometer should be

0.100 when the face of the measuring screw is in contact with the face of the plunger; the 0.100-inch mark is thus the zero line of this measuring tool.

When desiring to measure a number of pieces, a standard size piece or gage is placed between the plunger B and the face L of the micrometer screw, and the instrument is adjusted until the indicator points exactly to zero on the small scale provided on the body of the micrometer. After this the micrometer is locked, and the pieces to be measured are pushed one after another between the face L and the plunger B, the indications of the pointer M being meanwhile observed. Whenever the pointer shows too great a difference, the piece, of course, does not pass inspection. All deviations are easily detected, and any person of ordinary common sense can be employed for inspecting the work.

Micrometer Scale

A micrometer mounted as shown in Fig. 44 is very handy.

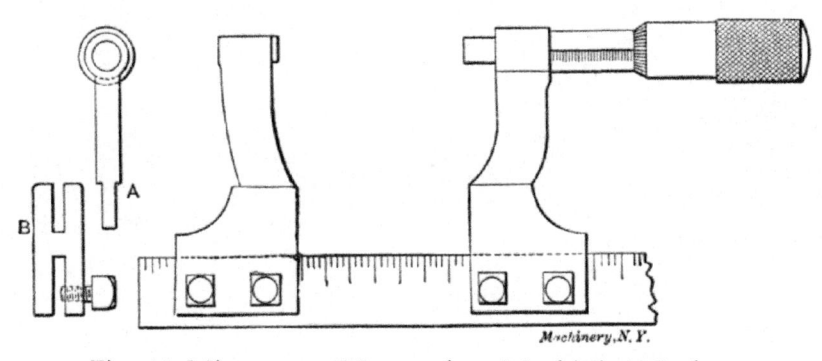

Fig. 44. Micrometer Mounted on Machinist's Scale

The micrometer may be used in combination with a 4-, 6-, 9-, or 12-inch scale. It can be adjusted on standard plugs, or one can make a set of gages up to 12 inches, out of 3/16-inch round tool steel wire, and use these for setting. In mounting the micrometer, before cutting it apart, mill the shoulders shown at A, and in milling the bottom pieces B, use a piece of machine steel long enough for both, cutting the piece in half after milling the slots. In this way one obtains perfect alignment. In a shop where a set of large micrometers is not kept, this arrangement is very useful.[22]

CHAPTER IV
MISCELLANEOUS MEASURING TOOLS AND GAGES

Among the miscellaneous measuring tools and gages dealt with in this chapter are tools and gages for measuring and comparing tapers, adjustable gages, radius gages, gages for grinding drills, sensitive gages, tools for gaging taper threaded holes, contour gages, etc. Of course, these are offered merely as examples of what can be done in the line of measuring tools for different purposes, and, while having a distinct and direct value to the mechanic, they also have a great indirect value, because they furnish suggestions for the designing and making of tools for similar purposes.

Tool for Measuring Tapers

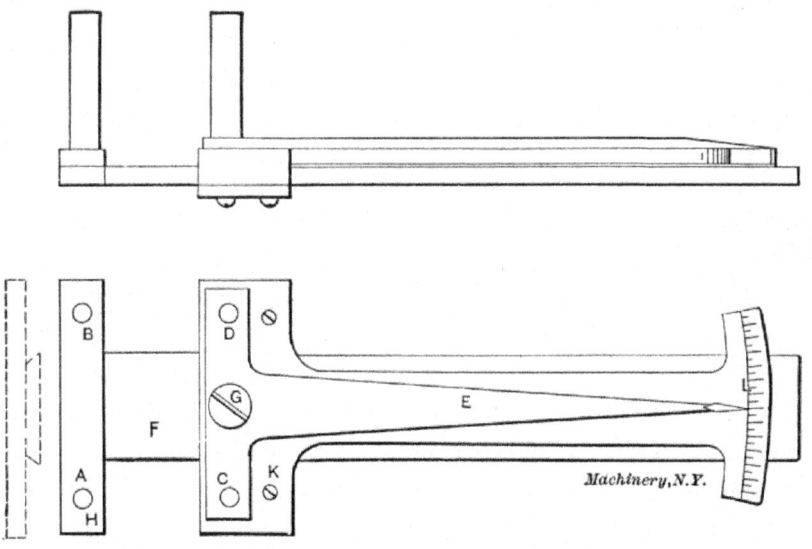

Fig. 45. Taper Measuring Tool

Fig. 45 shows a tool which has proved very useful. It is a tool for measuring tapers on dowel pins, reamers, drill shanks, or anything to be tapered. Most machinists know that to find the taper of a shank they must use their calipers for one end and reset them for the other end; or else caliper two places, say, three inches apart, and if, for instance, the difference should be 1/16 inch, they must multiply this difference by four to get the taper per foot. With the tool above mentioned, all this trouble in calipering and figuring is saved. Simply place the shank or reamer to be measured between pins A, B, C, and D, and slide H and K together. Then the taper can be read at once on the graduated scale at L. The construction of the tool will be readily understood. The body or base F has a cross piece supporting the two pins A and B. On this slides piece K, which has at its right end the graduated segment. The screw G is fast to piece K, and upon it swivels the pointer E, which carries the two pins C and D. Thus these two pins can be brought into contact with a tapered piece of any diameter within the capacity of the tool, and the swivel screw G allows the pins to adjust themselves to the taper of the work and the pointer E to move to the left or right, showing instantly the taper per foot.

As the pins A and B are 1½ inch apart, which is ⅛ of a foot, and the distance from G to L is 4½ inches, which is three times longer than the distance between A and B, the graduations should be 3/64 inch apart, in order to indicate the taper per foot in eighths of an inch.[23]

Taper Gage

A handy taper gage is shown in Fig. 46. The blades of the gage are made of tool steel. The edge of the blade A is V-shaped, and the blade B has a V-groove to correspond. The end of B is offset so as to make the joint and allow the two blades to be in the same plane. A strong screw and nut are provided to hold the blades at any setting. The user of this gage looks under the edge of A, and is thereby enabled to tell whether the taper coincides with that set by the gage, and also where a taper piece needs touching up to make it true.[24]

MEASURING TOOLS

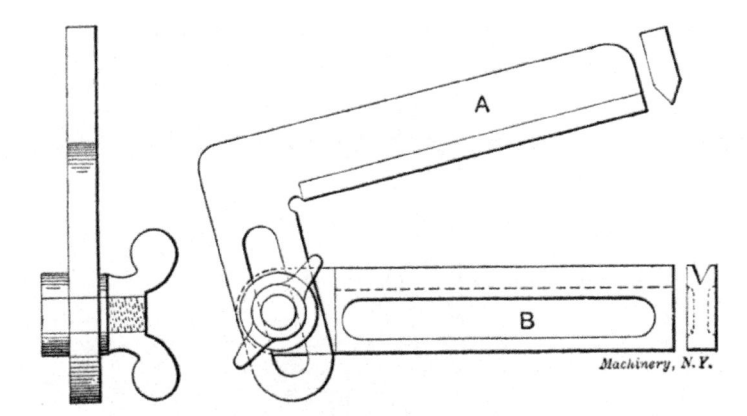

Fig. 46. Handy Taper Gage

Test Gage for Maintaining Standard Tapers

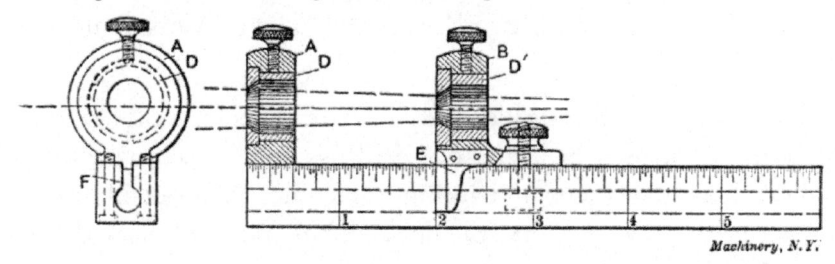

Fig. 47. Test Gage for Maintaining Standard Tapers

In steam injector work, accurately ground reamers of unusual tapers are commonly required, and the gage shown in Fig. 47 was designed to maintain the prevailing standard. It consists of a graduated bar, 1-inch square, with the slot F running its entire length. The stationary head A is secured in position flush with the end of the bar, and the sliding head B is fitted with a tongue which guides it in the slot. This head may be secured in any desired position by means of a knurled thumb nut. The bushings D and D' are made of tool steel, hardened and ground to a knife edge on the inside flush with the face. All bushings are made interchangeable as to outside diameter.

The head B is fitted with an indicating edge E which is set flush with the knife edge of the bushing. The reading indicates to 0.010

inch the distance the bushings are from each other, and the difference in their diameter being known, it is easy to compute the taper. With this gage it is possible to maintain the standard tapers perfectly correct, each reamer being marked with the reading as shown by the scale.[25]

Inside and Outside Adjustable Gages

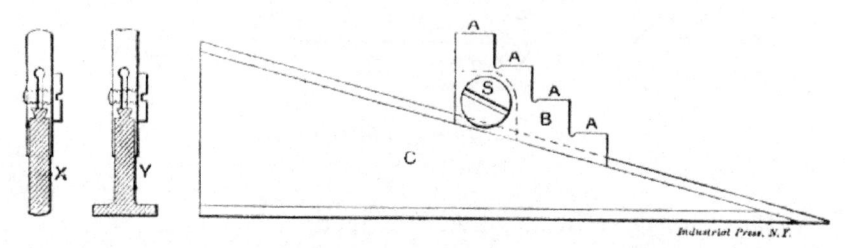

Fig. 48. Adjustable Gage for Inside and Outside Measurements

Fig. 48 shows an inside and an outside adjustable gage for accurate work, used in laying out drill jigs, and in setting tools on lathes, shapers, planers, and milling machines. The outside gage is shown in the side view and in the sectional end view marked Y. At X in the same figure is a sectional end view showing how the gage is constructed for inside work. The top and bottom edges are rounded, so that the diameters of holes may be easily measured.

The gage consists of a stepped block B, mounted so as to slide upon the inclined edge of the block C. There are V-ways upon the upper edge of the latter, and the block B is split and arranged to clamp over the ways by the screw shown at S. All parts of the gage are hardened, and the faces of the steps marked A, are ground and finished so that at any position of the slide they are parallel to the base of the block C. The lower split portion of the block is spring tempered to prevent breaking under the action of the screw, and also to cause it to spring open when loosened. The gage has the advantage that it can be quickly adjusted to any size within its limits, which does away with using blocks. In planing a piece to a given thickness, the gage may be set to that height with great accuracy by means of a micrometer caliper, and then the planer or shaper tool adjusted down to the gage. This method does away with the "cut-and-try" process and will bring the finishing cut within 0.001 inch of the required size. If the piece being planned, or the opening to be measured, is larger than the extreme limit of the gage, parallels may be used. In fitting bushings into bushing holes, the adjustable gage may be moved out to fit the hole, and then, when the bushing is finished to the diameter given by the gage, as determined by a micrometer caliper, a driving fit is ensured.[26]

Radius Gage

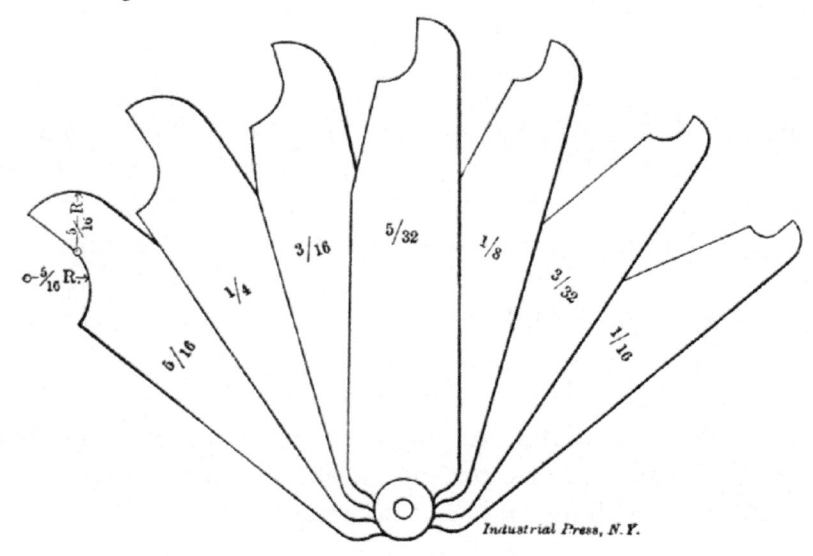

Fig. 49. Radius Gage

Fig. 49 shows a radius gage which has proved to be very handy for all such work as rounding corners or grinding tools to a given radius. The blades are of thin steel and are fastened together at the end by a rivet, thus forming a tool similar to the familiar screw pitch gage. The right-hand corner of each blade is rounded off to the given radius, while the left-hand corner is cut away to the same radius, thus providing an instrument to be used for either convex or concave surfaces. The radius to which each blade is shaped is plainly stamped upon the side.[27]

Gage for Grinding Drills

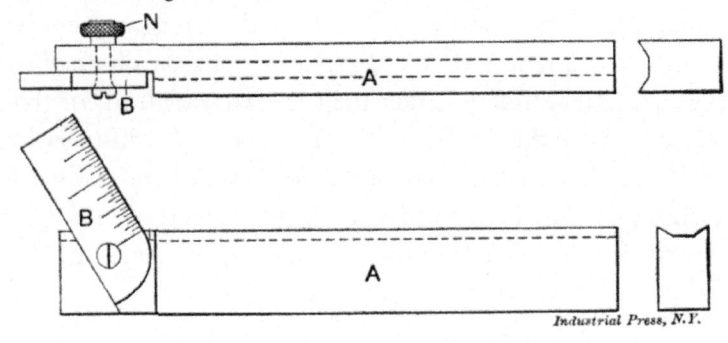

Fig. 50. Gage for Grinding Drills

Fig. 50 shows a gage for use in grinding drills, which has been found very handy and accurate. This gage enables either a large or small drill to lie solidly in the groove provided for it on top of the gage, and the lips can then be tested for their truth in width, or angle, much easier and quicker than with the gages in common use without the groove. There is a line, to set the blade B by, on the stock at an angle of 59 degrees at the top of the graduated blade, and the user can easily make other lines, if needed for special work. The blade is clamped in position by the knurled nut N at the back and can be thus adjusted to any angle. The stock A is cut away where the blade is pivoted on, so that one side of the blade comes directly in line with the middle of the groove.[28]

Tool for Gaging Taper Threaded Holes

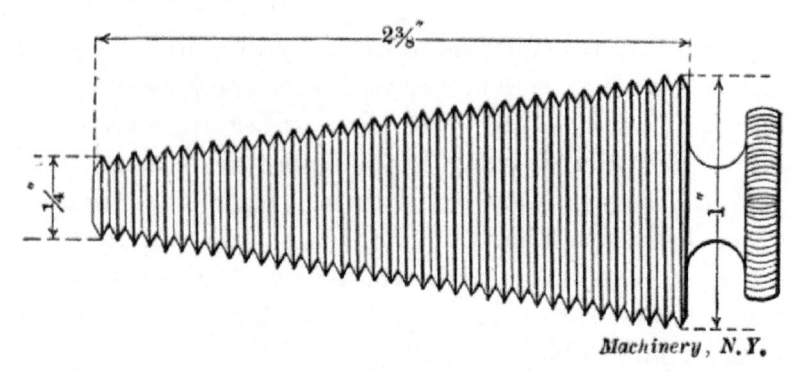

Fig. 51. Tool for Gaging Taper Threaded Holes

MEASURING TOOLS

The tool shown in Fig. 51 is used for gaging taper threaded holes in boilers when fitting studs. It is a simple, though very useful and economical tool, and it will doubtless be appreciated by those having much work of this kind to do. The hole in which the stud is to be fitted is calipered by filling the threads of the plug with chalk, and then screwing the plug in the hole. When the plug is removed the chalk will show exactly the largest diameter of the hole.[29]

Contour Gage

Figs. 52, 53 and 54 illustrate a special tool which will be found of great value in certain classes of work. The need of some such device becomes apparent when patterns and core boxes are required to be accurately checked with the drawings of brass specialties, in particular. The tool is applied to the work, and the wires pressed down onto the contour by using the side of a lead pencil. Of course, patterns parted on the center could have their halves laid directly on the drawing without using the contour gage, but some patterns are cored and inseparable. Such a tool proves a relentless check upon the patternmaker, who, by making the patterns larger than necessary, can cause a considerable loss in a business where thousands of casts are made yearly from the same patterns. As a ready and universal templet it is very useful.[30]

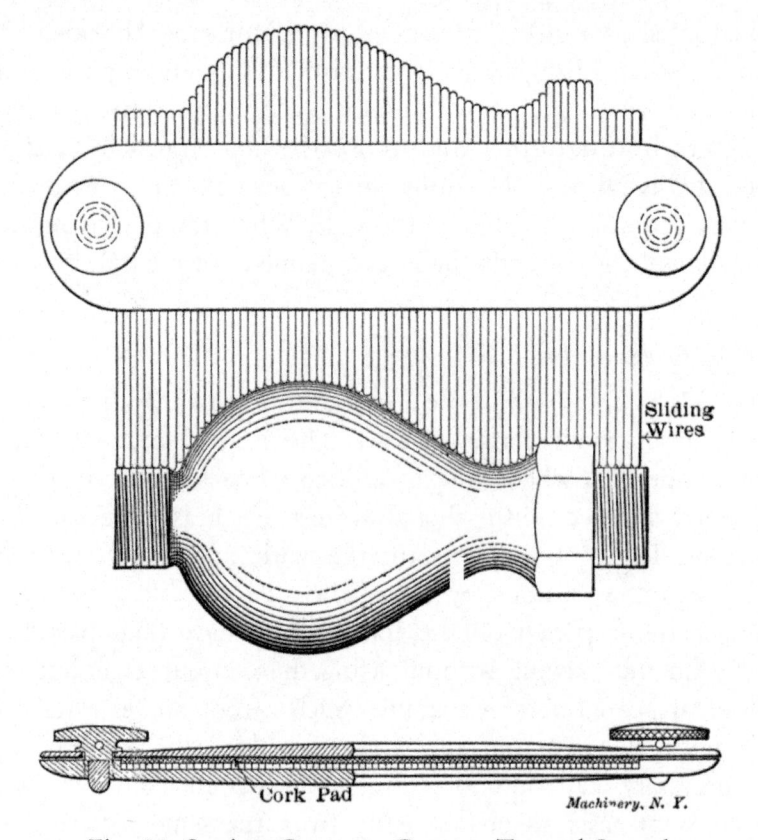

Fig. 52. Setting Contour Gage to Turned Sample

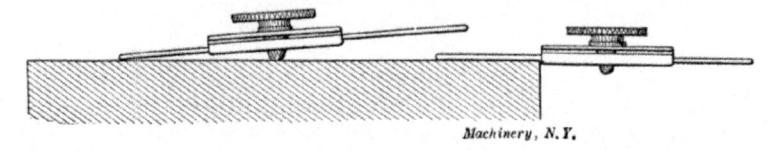

Fig. 53. End View of Contour Gage

A reliable way for testing the pitch of a lead-screw, at any position of its length, is to procure a micrometer screw and barrel complete, such as can be purchased from any of the manufacturers of accurate measuring instruments, and bore out a holder so that the axis of the micrometer screw will be parallel to the holder when the screw is in place, as shown in Fig. 55.

MEASURING TOOLS

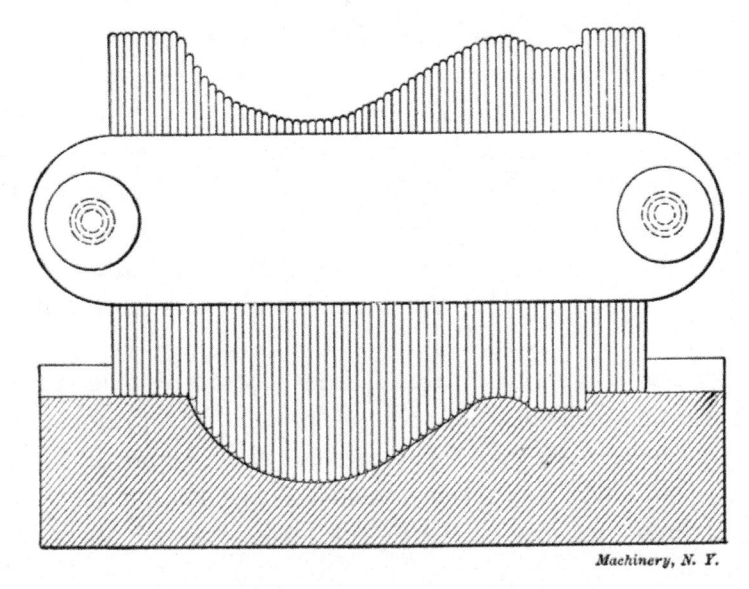

Fig. 54. Testing Core-box with Gage

Testing a Leadscrew

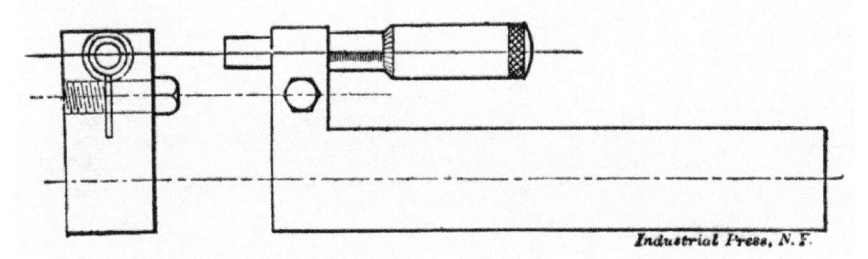

Fig. 55. Micrometer for Testing Lathe Leadscrew

With the lathe geared for any selected pitch, the nut engaged with the lead-screw, and all backlash of screw, gears, etc., properly taken up, clamp the micrometer holder to the lathe bed, as shown in Fig. 56, so that the body of the holder is parallel to the carriage. Adjust the micrometer to one inch when the point of the screw bears against the carriage and with a surface gage scribe a line on the outer edge of the faceplate. Now rotate the lathe spindle any number of full revolutions that are required to cause the carriage to travel over the portion of the leadscrew that is being tested, bringing the line on the faceplate to the surface gage point. If the distance traveled by the carriage is not greater than one inch, the micrometer will indicate the error directly. For lengths of carriage travel greater than one inch, an end measuring rod, set to the number of even inches required, can be used between the micrometer point and lathe carriage. The error in the leadscrew is then easily determined by the adjustment that may be required to make a contact for the measuring points between the carriage and the micrometer screw. The pitch can be tested at as many points as are considered necessary by using end measuring rods, of lengths selected, set to good vernier calipers. The style of holder shown can, with the micrometer screw, be used for numerous other shop tests, and as the screw is only held by friction caused by the clamping screw, it can easily be removed and placed in any form of holder that is found necessary.[31]

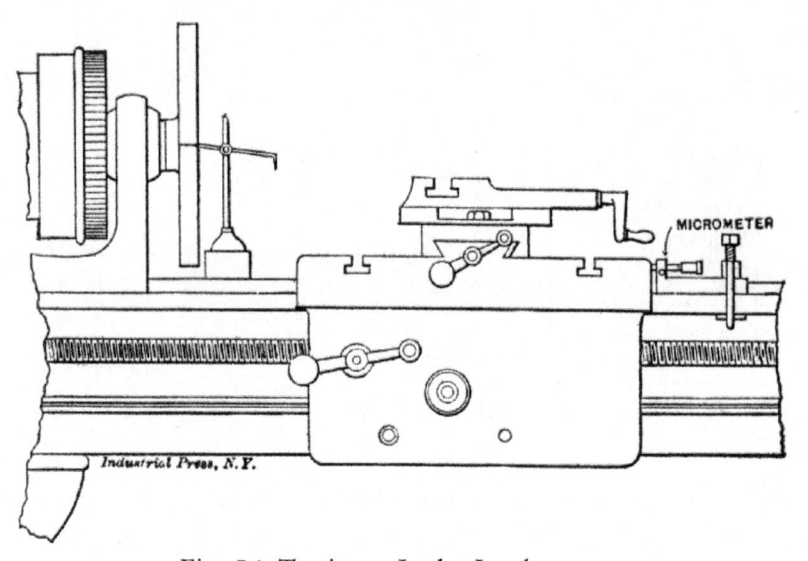

Fig. 56. Testing a Lathe Leadscrew

MEASURING TOOLS

Simple Tool for Measuring Angles

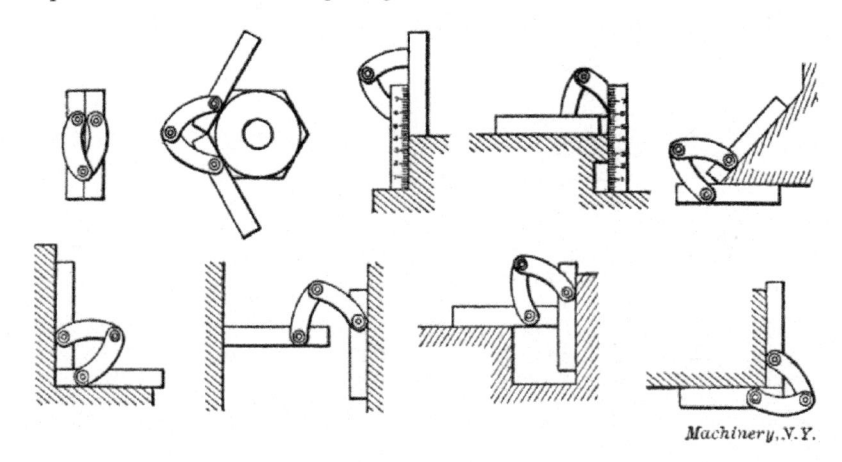

Fig. 57. Special Tool for Measuring Angles

Fig. 57 shows a very simple, but at the same time, a very ingenious tool for measuring angles. Strictly speaking, the tool is not intended for measuring angles, but rather for comparing angles of the same size. The illustration shows so plainly both the construction and the application of the tool, that an explanation would seem superfluous. It will be noticed that any angle conceivable can be obtained in an instant, and the tool can be clamped at this angle by means of screws passing through the joints between the straight and curved parts of which the tool consists. Linear measurements can also be taken conveniently, one of the straight arms of the tool being graduated. As both of the arms which constitute the actual angle comparator are in the same plane, it is all the easier to make accurate comparisons. This tool is of German design, and is manufactured by Carl Mahr, Esslingen a. N.

Bevel Gear-testing Gage

In Fig. 58 is shown a sensitive gage for inspecting small bevel gears. The special case shown to which the gage is applied in the engraving is a small brass miter gear finished on a screw machine, in which case some of the holes through the gears were not concentric with the beveled face of the gears, causing the gears to bind when running together in pairs. The gage shown is quite inexpensive, but it indicates the slightest inaccuracy.

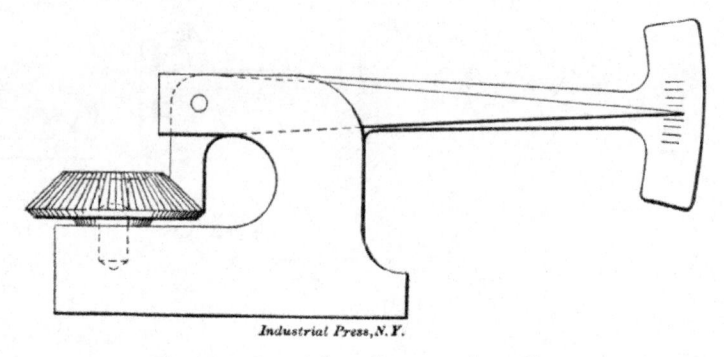

Fig. 58. Sensitive Gear-testing Gage

NOTES

[1] Machinery, October, 1897.
[2] M. H. Ball, April, 1902.
[3] M. H. Ball, February, 1901.
[4] Harry Ash, April, 1900.
[5] M. H. Ball, March, 1903.
[6] Ezra F. Landis, May, 1902.
[7] L. S. Brown, March, 1903.
[8] C. W. Putnam, October, 1901.
[9] Jos. M. Stabel, May, 1903.
[10] Jos. M. Stabel, May, 1903.
[11] Jos. M. Stabel, May, 1903.
[12] Jos. M. Stabel, May, 1903.
[13] P. L. L. Yorgensen, February, 1908.
[14] A. L. Monrad, December, 1903.
[15] A. L. Monrad, December, 1903.
[16] A. L. Monrad, December, 1903.
[17] J. L. Marshall, February, 1908.
[18] Charles Sherman, November, 1905.
[19] M. H. Ball, May, 1903.
[20] Chas. A. Kelley, May, 1908.
[21] H. J. Bachmann, December, 1902.
[22] Wm. Ainscough, May, 1908.
[23] John Aspenleiter, October, 1900.
[24] W. W. Cowles, June, 1901.
[25] I. B. Niemand, December, 1904.
[26] Geo. M. Woodbury, February, 1902.
[27] A. Putnam, July, 1903.
[28] M. H. Ball, October, 1901.
[29] F. Rattek, January, 1908.

[30] Howard D. Yoder,   December, 1907.
[31] W. Cantelo,   July, 1903.

Printed in Great Britain
by Amazon